"With a solid tie to research, this book makes g........ ..
parenting highly accessible and offers a million small ways parents
can promote their children's success. Where was this book when I
was a new parent?"

—Michele Borba, Ed.D.,
author of *UnSelfie* and *The Big Book of Parenting Solutions*

"We need parents who use their powerful influence to advance
kids' readiness for our global community. With that in mind, I
have advocated for and supported social and emotional learning
as fundamental to children's success. Jennifer Miller's book is an
essential guide for helping parents hone their own social and
emotional skills while helping their children do the same."

—Tim Ryan,
United States Congressman (OH-13) and author of *A Mindful Nation* and
The Real Food Revolution

"Jennifer Miller is a world-class expert in how to parent effectively.
This book is very informative, and I encourage parents to read and
re-read over the years as your children grow up. Jennifer provides
perspectives and practical strategies that will make parenting
experiences more enjoyable. They will also help parents to raise
happy, caring, responsible, and successful children."

—Roger Weissberg,
Leading Scientist in Children's Social and Emotional Development,
Chief Knowledge Officer for the Collaborative for Academic, Social, and
Emotional Learning (CASEL), and Distinguished Professor of Psychology
and Education at the University of Illinois at Chicago

CONFIDENT PARENTS, CONFIDENT KIDS

RAISING EMOTIONAL INTELLIGENCE IN OURSELVES AND OUR KIDS—FROM TODDLERS TO TEENAGERS

Jennifer S. Miller, M.Ed.

FAIR WINDS

Brimming with creative inspiration, how-to projects, and useful information to enrich your everyday life, Quarto Knows is a favorite destination for those pursuing their interests and passions. Visit our site and dig deeper with our books into your area of interest: Quarto Creates, Quarto Cooks, Quarto Homes, Quarto Lives, Quarto Drives, Quarto Explores, Quarto Gifts, or Quarto Kids.

© 2020 Quarto Publishing Group USA Inc.

First Published in 2020 by Fair Winds Press, an imprint of The Quarto Group, 100 Cummings Center, Suite 265-D, Beverly, MA 01915, USA. T (978) 282-9590 F (978) 283-2742 QuartoKnows.com

Fair Winds Press titles are also available at discount for retail, wholesale, promotional, and bulk purchase. For details, contact the Special Sales Manager by email at specialsales@quarto.com or by mail at The Quarto Group, Attn: Special Sales Manager, 100 Cummings Center, Suite 265-D, Beverly, MA 01915, USA.

24 23 22 21 20   1 2 3 4 5

ISBN: 978-1-59233-904-4

Digital edition published in 2020

eISBN: 978-1-63159-775-6

Library of Congress Cataloging-in-Publication Data available.

Design: Debbie Berne Design
Page Layout: Mattie Wells
Illustration: Jennifer Miller

Printed in China

To my confident partner, Jason.
To my confident son, Ethan.
To my confident parents,
David and Linda.
With all my love.

CONTENTS

Introduction 8

▮▮▮ PART ONE

UNDERSTANDING YOUR INSTRUMENT

1 The Jam Band 20
Two Truths and One Lie about Emotions

2 Melodic Themes 36
Better Understanding Your Child's Emotional Reflexes

3 Instrument Lessons 46
Methods for Building Social and Emotional Skills at Home

■ **PART TWO**

UNDERSTANDING YOUR CHILD:
PLAYING BY AGE AND STAGE

4 Rattles and Drums 64
Infants to 3-year-olds

5 Bass 90
4- to 7-year-olds

6 Guitar 110
8- to 12-year-olds

7 Horns 130
13- to 17-year-olds

■ **PART THREE**

UNDERSTANDING YOUR OWN INNER MUSICIAN

8 Self-Expression 156
Patterns, First Aid, Care and Maintenance, and Tone Tuning

Appendix 170

Bibliography 177

Acknowledgments 184

About the Author 185

INTRODUCTION

One day, my two-year-old son didn't want to stop playing. I had declared we needed to leave for an event. Red-faced and frustrated, angry and defiant, he lashed out with a mini-whack at my legs. I stared at him, shocked and dumbstruck while trying to hold back tears.

When he hit, I wanted to shrink away and cry. I felt hurt, like I had been punished. I also felt panicked. *What if he's going to become a violent person? How could I face that?* To further complicate my mounting emotional mess, I scolded myself because I knew these couldn't be honest predictions of his future. I thought, *How can I possibly react well to him in this situation when I feel so confused?* On top of this mash-up of hurt, panic, and guilt, I was frustrated because what I was feeling seemed irrational and much bigger than the situation actually merited. The diligent student of child development in me knew that my son did not have the language to express his anger—which is common in toddlers—so he lashed out to communicate. Why was my mind not informing my heart?

In my quest to answer this question, I set out on my own reflective journey. I knew I could react better, and I became committed to figuring out how I could respond with emotional intelligence in the future. How could I create teachable moments in my parenting? My search for answers required an unpacking of my own feelings to understand why I had such a fully loaded stack of emotions to an incident that, intellectually, I knew was developmentally normal—expected even—at my son's age.

That toddler-size hit woke me up to the fact that I had a lot to learn about raising a confident kid and becoming a confident parent. Though I had educated myself about my baby's physical well-being from the very moment I discovered I was pregnant, when my baby grew into a walking, talking toddler, I realized that there was much more to learn about my own emotional well-being—my confidence—as a parent.

I was intimately aware that my reactions to my feelings in times of challenge would become my son's emotional handbook. If I yelled, he would learn to yell. If I panicked, he would learn to panic. So, I became determined to learn all I could about promoting confidence in myself so that I could feel capable of building confidence in him.

Parents agree—confident is how we want to feel and act in our relationships with our families and what we want most for our kids. Specifically, we want our children to grow a belief within themselves that they can conquer any challenge with hard work and persistence, that they can love boundlessly, that they can

con·fi·dence

ˈkänfədəns/

noun

1. the feeling or belief that one can rely on someone; firm trust. "We have every confidence in you."
2. a feeling of self-assurance arising from one's appreciation of one's own abilities. "She's brimming with confidence."

find their unique sense of purpose, and that they can act wisely in a complex world. Our children trust that we will look out for their care and safety and make responsible decisions on their behalf. If we want to build confidence and these beliefs in our children, we have to trust that, as we allow for greater independence, they will increase their competence at each age and stage.

> "Specifically, we want our children to grow a belief within themselves that they can conquer any challenge with hard work and persistence, that they can love boundlessly, that they can find their unique sense of purpose, and that they can act wisely in a complex world."

What Is Confidence?

We develop a belief in each other's confidence as we demonstrate our competence. Ultimately, in order to hold that trust, we must increasingly learn to understand, accept, and express ourselves in alignment with who we are and what we deeply value, as well as understanding, accepting, and relating to others—namely, our children—as we seek to promote the best of who they are.

Confidence Is...

Confidence can take many shapes and forms from radical self-acceptance—flaws and all—to seeing the best in others, to tapping into a greater wisdom. Certainly, from culture to culture, the ways in which parents cultivate confidence in children will differ. Here are some simple examples I've observed in which confidence is demonstrated in parents' and children's lives.

- My ten-year-old son choosing to run track on a team with strangers because he loves the wind in his hair and the ability to challenge himself to go faster and farther. He chose this after years of playing baseball with all his friends and feeling the peer and community pressure that goes along with making a different choice.
- A client admitting to all-consuming worries about her kids' frenemies. Realizing that her fears influence how her kids learn to manage their relationships, she committed, with support from a parenting coach, to manage her anxiety and shift her reactions.

- A dad, who was raised to put down sensitivity and artistic expression as a male, choosing to promote and celebrate his son's early and continued interest in dancing ballet to grow trust.
- A mom known for her social connections and easy laughter—as outgoing as one can be—accepting and looking for ways to honor her son's extreme introversion in their daily encounters with friends, teachers, and other parents.
- A frequent commenter on the *Confident Parents, Confident Kids* blog recognizing and examining patterns learned from her own parents that were unhealthy and could creep into her parenting—intentionally or unintentionally. She continually educates herself on positive strategies to replace punishments such as yelling and spanking, despite the fact that her immediate friends and extended family continue to perpetuate those unhealthy patterns.
- A client's eight-year-old daughter with expected grade-level social and academic abilities befriending and including a marginalized student with significant and apparent social and academic challenges.

Confidence Is Not...

We often know confidence when we see it but struggle to define it or understand how to cultivate it. Are we born with it? Do some just have "it" while others do not? How do we know we are raising kids to become confident adults? Maybe it helps to look at what confidence is not.

- Confidence is not extroversion. It's not the loudest person in the room, the "life of the party," or the one who tells the funniest stories (though it can be).
- Confidence is not an individual who possesses the most power because he tromped on others, winning at all costs, to get there.
- Confidence is not a child who participates in the most extracurricular activities and it is not a parent who volunteers with her child's school the greatest amount of time.
- Confidence is not necessarily the person with the highest IQ, or the one who knows it all.
- Confidence is not found in the "A" papers a child produces or the awards a parent's work receives.
- Confidence does not require that a child or a parent control their emotions to the point of stuffing down, toughing out, or swallowing feelings to repress their expression.

The Beliefs of Confident Parents

Confidence exists in all shapes, sizes, colors, creeds, and cultures. In fact, confidence can be boiled down to a few underlying beliefs, all having to do with learning. To be confident, the following things must be true:

- You believe that learning and development are necessary and continual over a lifetime.
- You are humbled by the fact that there's much to still learn, that the term "perfect parent" does not exist.
- You trust in your kid's ability to learn (to make mistakes, to fall, to get up, and to make a better choice next time).
- You trust in your own ability to learn (to make mistakes, to fall, to get up, and to make a better choice next time).

These beliefs are a great start, but you may be wondering, *Is there any way to improve our confidence as a parent for the child we love? What if we weren't born unflappable?*

I'll be the first to tell you—I flap quite easily! If we weren't rattled and stressed before becoming a parent, the uncertainty and sheer responsibility of raising a human being introduces a whole host of new doubts, fears, and worries. So, how do we *gain* confidence?

I've spent the past seven years since my son's early childhood years trying to figure that out. And I did it by creating, expanding, and contributing to a learning community of others just like us, all of whom are finding simple ways to gain confidence in ourselves and our children.

Confidence Is Understanding and Managing Feelings

Let me bottom line it for you. It all comes down to understanding and managing feelings—both in ourselves and with our kids. And the great news is that, if we can build emotional competence in ourselves, we simultaneously build it in our children.

Here's evidence: Think about your greatest challenges with your children. Quick—name three. Now consider the following: Are feelings central to the challenge? In other words, did your child get angry in a store and throw a fit? Did your anxiety about your child's safety turn into yelling to impress upon him your point? Did your child lie about going to a friend's house and, when you found out, both you and she got so upset that it led you to your separate rooms with a considerable period of silence?

I posed this question to myself seven years ago: "Could small adjustments make a big difference over time?"

Confidence in parenting seemed like a monumental goal. I needed to break down how confidence could look, feel, and sound in parenting in small, practical ways. So I formed *Confident Parents, Confident Kids*, a blog where I could share weekly writings about simple, research-based ways parents could promote social and emotional competence in their kids, in an effort to help me become more reflective about my most important role as a mom. I hoped it might help others in the process too, and, to my great delight, it did. I heard from parents worldwide, from across the United States to distant countries such as Australia, South Africa, and China. They said, "We need more of this," and "When I try your small adjustments, I do feel more competent and confident!"

With this book, my goal is to provide supportive information that you can use right away to deepen your relationship with your kids *and* yourself. Remember those three challenges we discussed earlier? Write them down and save them to look back upon later. I guarantee that, at some point, your very challenge will be addressed in this book and, through your reading, you'll be ready to face it using practical strategies, ultimately gaining a greater sense of confidence.

When feelings are intense, words at times, cannot adequately describe what we're experiencing. That's where the arts come in. This book is steeped with illustrations and musical metaphors to engage our hearts and spirits as well as our minds. Learning about our own and our children's emotions is like learning to play a musical instrument. Our increasing awareness of and competence with our instrument—our feelings—allows us and them a vehicle for self-expression. If we want to harmonize with family members, attuning to each individual sound while producing an inspired song beyond the capacity of any one member, then we, as conductors of our band, need to lead the way.

Our feelings can become our greatest family assets, if we view them as vital messages from our brains and bodies to reflect what we or our children are experiencing. When we value our feelings by paying attention to them—not avoiding, rejecting, or ignoring them—we grow our self-awareness and, simultaneously, help our children grow their own self-awareness. When we make clear choices to calm down instead of yelling, for example, our children learn that they have choices, too, in managing themselves when they are angry or frustrated. And those choices can not only avoid harming those they care about but also strengthen relationships in the process.

In this book, you'll deepen your understanding of the critical role emotions play in your life. You'll learn simple ways to teach your children about their emotions so they gain a deeper sense of who they are and why they feel the way they do. You'll also begin to see the direct connection between how you manage your big feelings and your child's self-understanding, impulse control, and resilience.

> **"Building your emotional intelligence while learning about your child's development lessens anxiety and increases your sense of competence."**

For example, when a parent articulates her feelings—owns them, and reflects aloud on them—it teaches her child to do the same. You may say, "I felt frustrated and angry by your whining because you knew our rule about snacks before meals. But I shouldn't have yelled at you. Instead, I could have taken some deep breaths and then talked more calmly about it. Let me try again…"

This newfound self-awareness can extend your patience and demonstrate to children a positive way for them to constructively respond, as well as to own and reflect on their feelings. More importantly, it builds your own confidence in their responses at school and at friends' houses when you are not there to guide them.

A Parents' Confidence Saves a Life

To deeply understand, accept, and value another's unique heart is to forge a unity and demonstrate a love that is eternal. That is the parent's most sacred responsibility and privilege. The synchrony of our hearts with our children's can provide lasting physical and emotional strength.

Perhaps there is no better example than parents Katie and David. They tried for three years to conceive their first baby. So when they discovered they were having twins, they were overjoyed. At twenty-six weeks, Katie went into premature labor and was rushed to the hospital. At birth, their baby girl let out a big wail. But their son was born silent.

The doctors worked on their son with nurses and staff crowding in the room. Katie and David looked on with uncertainty and fear. After twenty minutes, their doctor said, "We've lost him." He had stopped breathing.

But Katie heard him gasp. She grabbed their baby from the doctor and ordered her husband to get in bed with them to warm their son with their body heat. Katie could tell their tiny boy was freezing. As she and David held him in a close embrace, she adjusted his ear to her chest so that he could clearly hear her heart beating.

"We told him he had a baby sister, and he needed to look after her," Katie recalled. "We had big plans for him, for his life. We made lots of promises."

And then, their son began to move. They called the midwives in with urgency. But the nurses just reiterated that he was dying and they needed to say their goodbyes. But Katie and David had no intention of saying goodbye. They held on and continued to tell him all about his extended family. Suddenly, their fragile boy opened his eyes, reached out, and grabbed the tip of David's finger, holding on for dear life. At that moment, they knew he would live.

Now eight years old, their son, Jamie, is known as Katie and David's miracle baby. He and his sister and their baby brother are all perfectly healthy. "Sometimes when I hug them, I think I hug a bit too tight," Katie said, "because I know how close I came to not having children."

The doctors point directly to their skin-to-skin embrace, which synchronized their heart beats, as the reason for Jamie's revival. Katie's and David's hearts acted as a regulator, assisting Jamie's heart with their own steady beats. It's also clear that their hope, confidence, and resolve—the power of their love—gave him the power to fight. They felt confident their love and support could bring their son back to life. And it did.

Researchers confirm that skin-to-skin contact and listening to and connecting heartbeats reduces stress and bolsters physical and mental resilience. And those benefits extend well beyond the baby years. In fact, our hugs, our comforting holds, and our tone of voice exuding hope and confidence continues to have a battery-charging effect on our children's nervous systems. As Katie and David showed, our commitment to our children and our demonstrations of love and faith that they can meet any challenge offer an emotional fortification like no other they may experience.

"Making the decision to have a child—it's momentous. It is to decide forever to have your heart go walking outside your body," wrote Elizabeth Stone, an author and educator. The emotions we experience in our roles as parents are some of the most highly sensitive, keenly felt in our lives. We feel responsible for raising a life. We feel the love, the worry, the empathy, and the hopes and determination, too, that come from being so invested in another person's well-being. And our sense of responsibility extends not only to ensuring that our children survive but also that they thrive.

Parents' Confidence Transforms a Life (and the World in the Process)

Pauline and Hermann exemplify how parents' confidence can not only help a child survive but also thrive in a world that may not recognize the gifts he has to offer. Their older son was born with a misshapen head. Family members worried that he would have developmental delays, a notion that was reinforced when he didn't speak, as his peers did, until he was three years old. Though extended family continued to perceive their son as challenged, Pauline devoted herself to teaching her son to play the violin and piano. She cultivated his love of the arts, and it became a vehicle for self-expression for this quiet child.

Convinced of his potential to learn but concerned schools might only see his limitations, Pauline homeschooled him until he was seven. When they felt pressured to send him to elementary school, Pauline frequently heard from his teachers that he would not participate and did not have the intelligence to meet their requirements. He endured punishment and humiliation at school for not paying attention and not answering questions correctly.

Their son also struggled with a temper and, when enraged, would throw things, sometimes directly at his younger sister's head. But both parents guided and encouraged him to be kind to his sister and look out for her. With their support, their son became more skilled at managing his anger and not harming others. He also became more kind and protective. When his sister became ill, Pauline and her son played duets to entertain her each evening.

Pauline and Hermann continually assured their son that they were certain of his competence. They intentionally sought out enriching opportunities for learning by inviting scholars over to their home for drinks and conversation. But Pauline and Hermann's son continued to struggle with traditional schooling. At fifteen, his teacher suggested he leave altogether. Despite this and numerous other setbacks, he managed to graduate from high school and college and then, rejected by his first attempts to find a professor position, made do working in a patent office. This man grew to become known as one of history's smartest men. This is the story of Albert Einstein and the confident parents who raised him.

PART ONE

UNDERSTANDING YOUR INSTRUMENT

THE JAM BAND

TWO TRUTHS AND ONE LIE ABOUT EMOTIONS

"Where words fail, music speaks."
—*Hans Christian Andersen, Danish fairy-tale author*

My client, Maria, came to one of our sessions with a pressing concern. "I got a call from Mrs. Wilson last night, Jesse's kindergarten teacher. She said Jesse has been 'losing it' in class. And other students have, too. But Jesse can't stop. She cries and cries. Mrs. Wilson said it takes a long time for her to recover and return to learning. She said it's taking time away from the class, disturbing other students. She told me I have to do something. What am I going to do? What if she gets suspended?"

I noticed Maria's pitch jumping higher into the soprano range as she asked that last question. I knew she was feeling panicky. I took a few deep breaths and responded slowly, reassuring her we'd work on it together. We discussed the facts of her daughter's situation. As a kindergartner, though she's becoming proficient in expressing her thoughts, Jesse is still learning to understand and express her feelings. She simply doesn't have the words for the all-consuming body takeover that occurs when she's upset, a feeling resembling the chaos of kids banging on instruments they don't know how to play.

Together, Maria and I attempt to piece apart the layers of Jesse's emotions. I asked, "How were your mornings on the day of the upset? Were they chaotic and stressful or smooth and connecting?" Maria considered and realized that, yes, more often than not, mornings are chaotic attempting to get two young children out of the door on time. That's one layer of feeling we uncovered—stress to start the day.

Other emotional layers emerged—Jesse's feelings of inadequacy when facing an academic challenge and of humiliation when she lost it in front of her class-mates and feared further ridicule. She likely sensed her teacher's disappointment and impatience with her. Every layer acted like one more ill-tuned instrument adding to the melee.

Even if Maria can learn skills to help quiet the emotional noise, how can she help her child self-soothe at school when she's not present? The key to helping Jesse internalize the skill was for Maria to offer regular practice opportunities at home by using feeling words to build her emotional vocabulary.

To keep this practice front of mind, Maria posted a list of words for emotions on the refrigerator—*frustrated, scared, excited,* for example—and each time Maria noticed a feeling on her daughter's face, she would name it and ask whether her label accurately described what was going on inside her. "Looks like you're feeling frustrated with homework. Is that right?"

In response, Jesse began to share with her mom what she was feeling more frequently. This offered valuable insight to Maria, who could lead Jesse to calm down in the early stages of her upset. The family even made a guessing game of emotions at dinner: "Let's see if we can tell what Dad's feeling when we ask, 'Dad, how was your day?'"

After two weeks of intentional practice using feeling words, Mom braced herself when she got a call in the evening again from Jesse's teacher. Mrs. Wilson began, "I don't know what you've done, but I have seen significant improvements in Jesse. She still gets upset but she recovers much faster. And when I go over to ask what's wrong, she tells me how she's feeling. It seems to calm her down as soon as she speaks." Maria relayed how they had worked on talking more about feelings at home. Jesse could communicate her emotions and she felt more understood when problems occurred.

As Maria hung up the phone, she felt awash with pride. She had faced a parenting challenge that had, mere weeks ago, felt insurmountable. Learning how to face it with emotional intelligence channeled her feelings into constructive action. She knew this experience would become the foundation for future challenges, allowing her to not only face them but harness them as teachable moments.

Jesse learned how to express the big feelings that were welling up inside of her. Like the jam band featuring every instrument at once, her emotions were all playing at the same time. Those individual notes of frustration, fear, and anger were lost in the noise. But with a little practice and encouragement in asserting her feelings, she became capable of helping others understand her. She had practiced the language of self-expression to make meaning of her internal upset.

Learning to Play Your Musical Instrument

If the vocal cords are the musical instrument of the body, emotions are the musical instrument of the heart, mind, and spirit. They give us quick feedback on our inner world in response to what's happening around us and inside of us. That information is vital to our survival. Like a trombone standing atop a bookshelf as a decorative piece, we may never learn to make music with it. But, if we develop our ability to play it, if we learn to express ourselves through it, our lives are nourished and enriched. We have a new voice through which to speak. That additional voice gives us a vehicle to more deeply connect with others while cultivating wisdom, marrying feelings with guiding principles. And wisdom is the highest form of confidence.

> "Children can learn about their emotions like they might learn a musical instrument."

The same is true for our feelings, whether tiny and subtle or engrossing and intense. Our continuous exploration of and reflection on our feelings offers us a wiser voice from which we can channel our parenting. Through that deep self-awareness, we are capable of greater intimacy with all those we love. And, in turn, we make greater meaning of our place in the world and our relationship to it. All those benefits become powerful modeling for our children, the most keen observers of our emotional reactions.

If learning about our emotions is like learning to play a musical instrument, we need to learn how to play the instrument ourselves first to be able to teach our children. As we more deeply understand the nuances and sensitivities of our instrument, we can discover a sense of joy, play, and mindfulness, as well as presence in the moment. As we experiment with varied techniques, we experience the beauty of mastering an instrument. We advance our musical intelligence just as we can advance our emotional intelligence. When we teach our children the basics of their instrument, not only are they ready but we feel authentic and competent as their teachers.

Interpreting Our Music

Emotions are instant interpretations of what is happening both outside and inside of us based on our past experiences. Through our feelings, we quickly make meaning of our circumstances. Just as we have to learn to make meaning from sentences, we have to learn to make meaning from our internal emotional cues. And our children, too, must decode the symptoms they feel in their bodies when they are upset. When they make the connection between those internal messages and how they can react to them in ways that nurture—rather than harm—relationships, they can begin to express what they feel inside. In our earlier example, Jesse discovered that her new voice, her ability to articulate her feelings, calmed her down because she felt understood.

Unlearning Myths about Emotions

Myths about the roles of emotions have become so embedded in our culture that we take them for granted. As a result, part of the learning we need to do requires unlearning.

Feelings: How Children Learn—Fact or Fiction?

Let's play "Two Truths and One Lie…" Have you played this game with your family? Below I offer two facts about emotions and one lie. The lies are common myths that we have to unlearn to become confident parents. Can you tell which is which?

1. As children, we come to understand our feelings through our interactions with others, especially our parents or central caregivers.
2. Children automatically figure out their feelings on their own as they develop.
3. The roles of feelings are taught in every school curriculum.

In fact, children do come to understand who they are (their sense of identity) and how they feel by the reactions of those most important others in their lives—parents, teachers, and friends. Most of what they learn about their own feelings comes in the form of modeling. They watch you as you go about your day. When you do something kind, like making soup for a sick neighbor, they take mental note that that's how you show compassion when someone you know is suffering. When you burn yourself on the stove, and recoil yelling, "OH #$%&*," they also learn that what you do when you get hurt is pull away and yell a cuss word to feel better. For better or for worse, our children learn through our everyday words and actions.

Children may reflexively cry when they get hurt. But your reaction to their hurt will determine their next move. Will they cry even more intensely if you look horrified? Will they move away to be alone if they feel you are judging them? If your daughter has crinkles between her eyebrows and a sullen expression, you may say to her, "You look worried." She then begins to make meaning of the sense in her body and the thoughts in her mind ascribing them to your word: *worry.* Whether we are unintentionally (as in the first example) or intentionally (as in the second example) teaching a child about her emotions, she is learning just the same.

> "Learning happens because of emotions, not in spite of them."

Feelings are taught in schools as well. Sometimes referred to as the hidden curriculum, feelings enter the classroom with our children and are integrally linked to their school experience. In fact, learning takes place because of emotions— because of your child's relationship with a trusted teacher, your child's feelings about the subject itself, and your child's relationships with peers.

Some schools do an excellent job intentionally teaching children about their feelings and ways to deal with them constructively through research-based social and emotional learning. These schools not only acknowledge that feelings are a part of being together as a class, they also teach children social skills, like how to collaborate, how to take another's perspective, and how to work through a thorny friend problem.

Many schools, however, are not intentional about emotions. Children still learn about feelings, albeit not necessarily the way you'd like them to. They may learn that crying is not allowed in gym class, that stress can't be shown during test-taking time (even though it's wholly felt), and that grand expressions of joy should only happen on the playground.

In the 1940s, studies were conducted with children raised in U.S. orphanages who sadly received little interaction with caregivers. The researchers compared these babies with another institution—babies who were raised in a prison nursery with their imprisoned mothers. The first group in the orphanage was fed and changed on a timely schedule but had little interaction with caregivers. Those infants showed signs of significant emotional disturbance and developmental delays. In fact, the lack of interaction with others led to a lack of physical, cognitive, and emotional growth and one in three died before age two. But the babies in the prison who spent time with their mothers each day fared far better. They were healthier with normal emotional development and every one of them lived.

Let's look back at our two truths and a lie. Did you guess correctly? Sentence two is a lie. Children do not automatically learn about their feelings. They require the direct connection and loving interactions with you to learn about themselves and their emotions. And though this example is from the baby years, as you will discover in chapters 4 through 8, children continue to develop and learn about their identity and emotions into their young adult years just as adults continue to learn.

Feelings: Simple or Complex?

Let's play again! Here are a couple more truths and one lie. This is a tricky one!

1. Feelings are basic, easily identifiable, and one-dimensional. For example, we typically feel only happy or only mad.
2. We can mask, or hide, what we are feeling inside.
3. We have multiple feelings at once, sometimes conflicting.

Researchers are discovering that emotions are more complex than we once thought. Though our son may feel happy when he ties his shoes correctly, he'll surely feel a different kind of happy when he is given a new toy by his grandmother. We can teach feelings to young children as basic—happy, sad, mad—but in reality, we can better consider those as categories of experiences. (Statement 1 is a lie but can feel true at times, especially since feelings are often taught as one-dimensional.)

Neuroscience researchers verify this information by watching varying patterns (not the same) light up on imaging scans (fMRIs) for what might be considered "happy" depending upon the context—what the person experiences at the moment. What does this mean for us? Two things: There's much to learn about our own feelings and the feelings of our children and, secondly, the environment and experiences we create for our children matter greatly in how they develop.

As parents, we frequently fall into the role of feelings' detectives. We realize that if we don't get to the root of what's going on, it will carry on and fester. So we have to search for clues. It can be quite a challenge, as feelings emerge not only from external forces but internal ones as well, whether it relates to worries about a future event or an empty stomach. Parents know "hangry" (anger plus hunger) is a real emotion.

Take, for example, my client Cynthia's experience with her son, Toby, at the start of fourth grade. After dropping off Star Wars stickers with his teacher to share with each classmate in celebration of his tenth birthday, Cynthia received the most penetrating stink eyes from her son. After school, Toby expressed his fury with her by not talking the whole length of the car ride home. The only words he muttered before running to his bedroom were "Star Wars stickers are so stupid, Mom." She could hear him crying through the door and left him alone to cool off.

When she described the story to me, she ended with, "I just know he couldn't get that upset over stickers." She had only guesses. Did the kids tease him about the stickers? Was he embarrassed by his love of Star Wars? I told her she was likely right that there was more to it and challenged her to find out what was really going on for him.

A few days later, while having an after-school snack with Toby, Cynthia brought up the sticker incident. "I felt like there was more to the story. Can you tell me what you were feeling that day?"

Toby's face turned a shade of pink and his eyes watered. "I know I'm supposed to be happy about double digits, but I don't want to turn ten. I want to stay nine."

"Oh, I so get that," mom said with a sigh of empathy, having just hit her fortieth birthday, and relief at finally getting to the bottom of the issue. This discussion brought them closer together. She better understood Toby, and he felt more fully understood by his mom.

We can hide our feelings, even—and most especially—from ourselves. We may create diversions or excuses to explain away our big feelings, as in the sticker incident. And we tend

> "Because adults and kids alike can become adept at hiding feelings, we have to reflect, listen to our inner hunches, and follow up with them to learn what's really going on."

to do an extra thorough job of masking those feelings that are more painful or may not seem fixable, like the fear of getting older.

Toby felt utterly disappointed in himself for not feeling happier over the milestone birthday, masking it with anger and hurt over the stickers his mom brought to school. We all have moments of conflicting feelings, but, for children, the experience of that internal paradox can be confusing. However, they are far better able to understand and deal with that conflict if their parents are emotionally intelligent enough to reflect back to them those emotions. "It's such a strange experience when you feel happy—or others tell you that you should feel happy—but you feel sad too, isn't it?" With those words, we help deepen their self-awareness, and they learn to become more self-compassionate.

Feelings: Symptoms? Strength or Weakness? Shut-Off Valve?

How are you doing with our game? I'll give you a few more chances to guess. And yes, they're getting trickier! The next two truths and a lie are:

1. Our bodies show symptoms of our feelings, particularly our bigger feelings.
2. The better we can understand, name, and explain our feelings, the stronger, more flexible, and more resilient we become.
3. Feelings have a shut-off valve. If we are told to stop crying or feeling sad, we are capable of shutting it down quickly.

What's your "tell" when you are anxious or upset? Do you have a visible body sign? My husband and son get red ears that show they are tired or stressed, or both. Emotions are signals from the brain and body that combine electrical pulses and chemicals in reaction to external and internal experiences and thoughts. These reactions can automatically trigger facial expressions, vocalizations, and body postures to instantly show what we are feeling. Candace Pert, a neuroscientist responsible for significant discoveries in the connections between mind and body, explained it this way: "As our feelings change, this mixture of peptides travels throughout your body and your brain. And they're literally changing the chemistry of every cell in your body." In this way, we are like a living battery projecting these electrical pulses of emotion beyond our body to those around us. This wave of feeling produces nonverbal communication well before we can utter a word.

Body Language Does Not Lie

Did you know that body language has five times the impact that words have and can reveal a host of feelings? We can tell if children are lying, for example, when they cover their mouths with their hands. Even teens and adults, when saying something untrue, will place a finger near their mouth, as if to cover it up.

"I was raised to believe that feelings equaled weakness," my client Vivian told me as we began to work together. "If you had a negative feeling, you had to hide it. Strong people toughed it out. So when my children get upset, my instinct is to think, *Get over it*." Vivian wanted to extend her patience. She wanted to become more empathetic to her children's feelings, but her childhood beliefs continued to show up as she faced her children's big emotions.

Children cannot shut down feelings. None of us can! Feelings do not happen to us passively but are an important, proactive way we make meaning of the world. Biologically, they are rigged for our survival, and they are messages that won't be ignored, stopped up, or shoved down. Consider then that telling your child to "shut up" their feelings is rejecting their heart, mind, and spirit. Likewise, forcing yourself to stuff down your feelings is rejecting your own heart, mind, and spirit.

Take a moment to think of the last time you tried to not feel what you were feeling. Maybe you got mad or felt hurt and just didn't have time for the pain, so you attempted to stop it. What happened? Were you able to shut it down? If you played the distraction game and watched a movie or read a good book, did the feelings return at any point? And when they came back, were they

"Resilience comes from honoring feelings, not burying them."

stronger? Feelings can be temporarily "shelved," but your heart, mind, and spirit are attempting to communicate with you and will indeed get louder and more persistent because they are not being heard.

Imagine your young child repeating, "Mom, Mom, *MOOOOOOM!*" Like your child, your feelings work hard to get your attention, and they have to turn up the intensity at times to get you to listen. That's why understanding our emotional needs and how we can support them contributes to our resilience. We can prioritize meeting these needs and, when we do, we feel more capable of riding the waves of challenging times. Once we have a handle on that, we can then help our children do the same. Specifically articulating mixed emotions helps our children understand themselves better. They begin to better trust themselves and we can become more confident in our reactions to them. If we ignore their feelings, they will return louder, and we will face a feelings thunderstorm rather than a mild rain shower.

Raising a confident, strong, and resilient child—one who can face adversity and come through it wiser rather than beaten—requires that she deeply understands the perceptions of her heart, mind, and spirit. She will hear their messages and decide how she wants to interpret them through her choices. Instead of placing blame, she can ask, "What can I control or influence? How can I make a better next decision, and how can I learn from this?" There will be no need to apologize for her authentic feelings and associated needs. She will become capable of articulating where she stands in the world and how she perceives it so that she can voice her needs, desires, and passions with skill and flexibility. And, while you cannot protect her from all the dangers and pains of the world, you can feel confident that she will have had that invaluable practice at home of being able to articulate her needs. This child has learned to play a musical instrument, her feelings' voice tuned and ready.

Feelings: Irrational? Historical? Contagious?

Okay, ready for the last round of two truths and a lie? It's the trickiest of all. I'm switching it up and giving you four statements. Decide which ones are facts and which are lies.

1. Feelings cannot be trusted. They can be irrational and nonsensical.
2. Feelings can emerge from past experiences and from our own childhood, even if we don't recall in the moment the connection to that history.

3. Emotions are contagious.

4. There are negative emotions we need to reject, such as anger or fear, and positive emotions to embrace, such as feeling proud or comfortable.

Feelings have often been misunderstood because of their complexity. Some people consider feelings untrustworthy, not to be consulted for decision-making. And certainly, when we have a strong feeling, it's an intuitive snap judgment of what's happening around us. After the thought enters in, we may find that our feeling was urging us to an action for which our rational mind disapproves. "Yell at him!" our feeling urges. "No, don't! It'll only make things worse!" our rational mind volleys back.

These instant interpretations decide what information around us is important and focuses in on just that impression. For example, if our toddler takes off running in a supermarket, our instant reflex to run after him serves us well. But, as we know, first impressions don't contain all of the information we need to make responsible decisions. When our two children are fighting with one another, and we enter the picture moments later, the guilty-looking child may feel greater responsibility, even if he's not the instigator. That's why reflection about the meaning and purpose behind our feelings is critical.

Because emotions are information from our minds and hearts that are based on past experiences, they are indeed reasonable. Imagine this scenario: Tony's toddler son drew in indelible black ink on the freshly painted wall. Rationally, Tony knows he can find a way to clean up the mess, that his toddler is merely creating art and not acting out to spite him. But if anger arises and sends Tony the message to physically express it by throwing a lamp across the room, Tony may find that feeling to be unreasonable. However, past values and beliefs may be generating his anger. He may have watched his own father throw a lamp in anger. He may have been raised to take pride in his home and invest in it with hard work. He may have also been raised with parents who felt that any poor choice, even an accident, was a sign of disrespect. For Tony, the reaction that the emotion prompts is inappropriate based

> "Feelings may point us to an inappropriate action. That's why reflection is essential, so that we make choices that align with our core values."

on his current context and values. He doesn't want to scare his son by throwing a lamp. But he learned the feelings, values, and beliefs associated during his own childhood in a different time and place with different values. Even so, he faces managing those big feelings just the same (more on this in chapter 8). His challenge now is to learn how he can align his actions with his current values while also managing his emotions in healthy ways.

This concept is not always easy to accept. Consider how we fight the conclusion that our feelings are rational, considering our past. Your internal voice says, "What's wrong with me?! Why am I so mad?" Tony had that very thought when he witnessed his son's wall art. As parents, we easily beat ourselves up for feeling strongly in the moment or in reflection after an incident. Especially since our most intense emotions in life tend to relate to our children.

In a world where many believe the myth that feelings equal weakness, expressing ourselves vulnerably means we are showing our weakest side to our kids. And in a world where parents are supposed to be perfect for their kids (another myth), this seems completely unacceptable. In that world, big feelings should not be allowed. But as you are learning (or unlearning!), this just cannot be. In fact, our self-bashing contributes to the problem; it reduces our patience and adds to our internal upset volcano that is bound to erupt—and never in a convenient moment (not that there is one) and certainly it will happen in front of our precious children. In fact, our children can only learn to manage their big feelings constructively with our modeling and guidance.

What does it mean to trust our feelings? It means to listen to the gut feeling within us. In our earlier example with the mom, the son, and the Star Wars stickers, the mother did not initially trust her hunch that her son's feelings were about more than just the stickers. It took my pushing for her to return to the conversation and find a way to communicate with her son about it. We miss some of the wisest parenting counsel from our very own inner guidance when we ignore our feelings.

Through the natural course of our children's development, as they necessarily test limits and make mistakes in order to learn, their difficulties can elicit emotional memories from our own childhood. When our child acts out and we have a reaction that feels irrational—bigger than the situation actually merits—that is our first clue that emotional memories have been triggered. The mysterious part of this reaction is that we don't typically recall the story or the context of the memory involved, just the feeling. Why does this happen? Because feelings make meaning of today's circumstances based on our past experiences, and that includes any part of our past.

What leads you to a place of feeling irrational? When have you felt those feelings in your past? What values and messages did you learn at a young age that may relate to your current feelings about your parenting challenges? Reflecting on these connections can produce empowering revelations about yourself and help

> "Parent-child hugs prevent illness and promote trusting connections."

you face your child's challenges with your eyes wide open. Chapter 8 provides more opportunities to explore these questions.

Feelings *are* contagious, and that has major implications for our parenting. Have you ever listened to a friend who was tearing up while recalling a painful story and found yourself welling up with tears despite the fact that you weren't involved and hadn't felt sad at all that day? You're not alone. In fact, we are born with a reflex to mimic others' feelings. Researchers claim it is the very foundation of empathy. That mimicry can take place in various parts of the body and through a variety of expressions including:

- **Facial expressions.** Even when individuals were unaware they were mimicking another expression, researchers could track subtle changes in the muscles of the face that perfectly matched the other person. Blushing and yawning are two other examples of faces sharing emotions.
- **Eye contact and pupil dilation.** Research has shown that more direct eye contact between a mother and her child increases both heartbeats and the ability to understand the other's emotional experiences. When eye contact is made, pupils dilate to the same diameter, matching one to the other.
- **Skin-to-skin contact.** Hospitals often promote skin-to-skin contact between a mom and her newborn. Did you know that loving touches like hugs between parents and children and teenagers (all ages, not just babies) can boost immunity, reduce stress, and create a greater sense of trust and well-being?
- **Heart rate.** Just as with skin-to-skin contact, and perhaps part of the power of that connection, heart rates of individuals experiencing the same emotions will sync up with one another. This has been tracked with people watching movies or experiencing a compelling speaker. Consider the implication that

your heartbeat syncs up with your family members at dinnertime—or during a heated family argument.

- **Crying.** Maybe you've experienced babies who begin crying when another in the room cries. Even day-old infants do this. And, interestingly, the crying intensity, tone, and quality precisely mimics the others.
- **Brain activity.** As seen in fMRI studies, when emotions are expressed by one person, the same patterns of neural firing happen in the observing person's brain. This has been tracked with emotions such as fear, pain, disgust, reward, anxiety, envy, and embarrassment.

These ways our body mimics the feelings of others don't have to turn into full-blown emotions every time they occur. But emotional contagion is real and is influenced by the intensity of the feelings expressed by others. The more intense, the more likely we are to catch the feeling and fully experience it.

If daddy comes home sullen and grumpy from his workday, we'll not only feel his energy but we may also become more irritable with one another as we catch his mood. Or perhaps our child becomes smoking angry at mom for what might be viewed as a tiny, insignificant incident (for example, she forgot to buy his peanut butter crackers). He then sinks into a heap on the floor crying. When he finally calms down enough to speak, mom learns that he was pushed and called names at school. She feels genuine pain and worry as she empathizes with her hurt child—and when his younger sister comes into the room whining, she snaps at her.

You can also use the fact that feelings are contagious to your advantage. For instance, you can stop yourself from fanning the flames when you feel you are catching a grumpy mood you don't want to catch. You could take a walk outside for some fresh air and a fresh perspective to alter your energy. You may stop and take some deep breaths, knowing the power of breath to change both your internal and external states of mind.

In attempting to change the family energy, play can offer a source of diversion and mood change for all. Simply hitting a balloon and keeping it up in the air together can shift tension from a dinner filled with angst to family members who begin to smile, laugh, and cooperate. Consider that your hug, expression of love, and warm smile before your child leaves for school in the morning may just create the ideal conditions for his learning. Children learn best in a safe, caring environment with trusting relationships and the confidence that they can learn anything with time and hard work. Your feelings of love and support right before sending your daughter to school can offer a positive emotional contagion to set the tone for her day. Have a teenager who is regularly declaring her independence? Tweens and teens still need and value your expressions of love and support, though it may need to happen in the privacy of your home rather than in public in front of their peers.

Finally, can we judge emotions as negative or positive? Do we need to stop some immediately while promoting others? Particular feelings, like anger and disgust, have gotten a bad reputation and have been labeled "negative" emotions. Our tendency may be to believe they're undesirable and that we need to shut them down. And we have good reason to feel this way. Most of us have experienced someone who has made destructive choices when they felt out of control, certainly an experience we want to avoid. But these emotions can more accurately be considered threat or warning signals and prepare us for danger or alert us to injustice. All emotions are biologically wired with a positive intention—to send us a vital message about ourselves: our beliefs, our understandings, our boundaries. The key then becomes the meaning we make of those messages.

Emotions, Parenting, and Our Children's Success

What do emotions have to do with our parenting? The short answer: everything. They impact every aspect of our roles. Just as music seals in memories (I'll bet you can remember a song from your high school prom and certainly from your wedding!), so, too, do our emotions.

Consider the memories you are making now with your child. Now think about the fact that the memories your child will recall are those infused with feeling from the most loving, intimate times to the most upsetting, frightening, or sad occasions. How we react in all of those times determines whether or not our children will feel the support and love we want them to in order for them to thrive now and in the future. Isn't it worth our investment to spend a little time figuring out how we can respond in ways that harmonize with family members by bringing our wisest, most confident selves?

> "Emotions seal in memories for ourselves and our children."

MELODIC THEMES

BETTER UNDERSTANDING YOUR CHILD'S EMOTIONAL REFLEXES

"Melody is pure intuition." —*Sia, Australian singer/songwriter*

"I assumed my child would be like me," said Annette, reader and contributor to the *Confident Parents, Confident Kids* blog. "But as he grew, I began to discover he wasn't like any other." Annette felt a major growth spurt for her as a parent was when she came to the realization that her son, Brady, was not who she thought he *should* be. Her discovery came about as she examined challenges with her son in everyday activities. She described buzzing through the grocery checkout line, chatting with the cashier, offering insights about the weather, and complimenting her hair ribbon or his warm smile. Yet, at her side, her son was hiding. And as his mom insisted he come out from hiding and say "hello," smile, and be polite to the cashier, he cried with sadness, feeling misunderstood, a tinge of anger at the injustice plus an urgency to return to hiding.

At playgroups, she recalled longing for her son to play with others as much as she wanted to connect with other adults. At the end of the school day at pick-up time, she wanted him to recount every social interaction of the day. In response, Brady would just shut down or get upset as her insistence increased. "I remember feeling judged, like a failure, and upset with my son. I knew it was my ego, but it was crushing every time." Annette recalled frequently apologizing for his behavior to others until a pivotal event rattled her, like listening to a singer unable to hit a note on pitch.

One day, while playing on the playground with friends, Brady made a wise decision to not climb on top of a cement wall on the playground, despite the fact that his peers had and a playgroup parent was playfully daring them to do it. Annette, in an attempt to save social graces, sided with the adult friend and apologized for her son. That moment was a wake-up call for Annette.

"Why was I not sticking up for my son? What was that teaching him?" she reflected later. "I wanted affirmation that I was parenting him well. I was looking for it in his performances with others rather than in who he actually was."

She began to read about introverted children, how they experience the world differently than an extroverted individual, and what they need emotionally and practically. Through her research and reflections, Annette examined how her son encountered life in his unique way. She stopped apologizing to others for his quietness and, instead, worked on accepting his tendency to withdraw from new persons and situations, to require time to adapt, and to experience novelty in thoughtful silence.

"My goal is to empower him to live the way he needs to live. The only way for me to do that is to abandon my idea of how my child should reflect my mothering. I continue to learn about how he feels about the world, and I try to support him in expressing this experience in the way he needs to."

A Child's Melodic Theme: Temperaments

Temperaments tend to be the melodic theme of a child. What's the typical mood of their song? How do they react to new people, places, or challenges? You may intuitively sense that your child was born to approach situations by confronting them head on with curiosity or by backing away and observing. Babies are born with a consistent way of immediately responding to new people and situations, much like an emotional reflex. This part of your child's personality is considered foundational but also can be shaped by their environment, just as a default setting on your computer can be changed to fit a user's preferences.

Indeed, we are all born with a certain set of temperaments. As we grow, we choose our reactions so we can learn to react differently than our initial feeling might suggest. But these tendencies do not change because a parent scolds them out of a child. Children may have to change their reactions to fit social situations, but the feelings they initially experience will be consistent and stable over time. If a child is scolded for their reactions related to their temperament, it can lead to stronger emotions, like when Brady would cry or get angry because he felt his mom's disapproval. Brady likely felt shamed, guilty, and unsure of how to proceed. Parenting that ignores or reprimands a child for his temperament is a predictor of increased fear and upsetting reactions. Conversely, parenting with higher levels of warmth, sensitivity, and responsiveness to a child's temperament can decrease his upsets and outbursts.

Temperaments can be a significant source of conflict in a family. Since no two children are exactly alike—and, in fact, temperaments can and will differ widely between siblings—the differences in reactions can create friction. And, as

"Each child is born with a set of unique emotional tendencies that may differ from other family members."

in Annette's example, it's common that there may be differences in temperaments between a parent and her child, adding to frustrations when cooperation or even safety are at stake.

Each temperament, though, has a positive intent: to support your child's survival and development. From the most cautious child who may be saved from danger because of his risk aversion to the persistent child who stays so focused on his playing you cannot divert him from the task at hand, if you identify these specific temperaments, you can discover how they can serve as an asset to your child. This focus allows you to treat your child's emotional reflexes as strengths you can support and from which you can build social and emotional competence.

Discovering Your Child's Emotional Reflexes

How do you know what your child's temperaments are? And how do you distinguish between a consistent temperament and developmental changes that will come and go with various ages and stages? It's time for a quiz to find out. Get out your pencil and jot down your responses. The end result will be a temperament profile for your child. Be sure you go through the whole set of questions for each child in your family, since each child will be different. Also, to see how you might be similar or different from your children (which can inform your choices in parenting), each question in this quiz starts with a question for you to think about your own initial reactions. It's helpful for you to figure out where your tendencies and approaches are similar and different from each of your children.

1. Your boss has hired a team of ten new people to lead a project on which you'll need to coordinate efforts. She's hosting a get-to-know-the-new-team happy hour. When you receive the invitation, do you feel excited looking forward to meeting the new team or are you anxiously dreading it? Do you tend to *approach* new people or situations with interest or do you *withdraw*, cautiously backing away from strangers or new environments? Responses will vary on your own or your child's initial fear or inhibition (wanting to pull away) reaction. Now, think of a time recently when your child (no matter what age) met a new person. Was he or she eager or curious to meet the new person or did he or she hang back, a bit reluctant to approach?

Now consider when your child was a baby. Can you recall how your infant reacted to new people, places, or objects? Did she cry? Was she fearful? Or was she interested and eager to explore? On a scale of 1 to 5, with 1 being the most fearful of new people and situations and 5 being the most curious and interested in new people and situations, how would you rate your child?

2. If you've ever tried to learn a new instrument, were you *patient*, or did you get *frustrated easily?* Parents and children can also vary on how quickly they get frustrated or irritated when trying something new. We all get frustrated when we struggle with learning a new task, but temperaments are about initial reactions. Some children will work on a new task a bit until they get frustrated while others will work on it without irritation until they have mastered it. On a scale from 1 to 5, with 1 being the most quickly irritated and frustrated and 5 being the least and most eager to tackle a challenge, how does your child tend to react?

3. Do you smile or get excited when a new song plays on your favorite radio station, or do you wait cautiously to see if you'll like it or change to something more familiar? What tends to be your *go-to mood?* Parents and children also have different tendencies toward receptive reactions, like smiling, laughing, and an eagerness to check out new things. Does your child show pleasure when exploring new things? Does he smile and laugh easily? Or do new people, places, or things incite cautious concern, irritation, or even upset? Where would you place your child on the 1 to 5 rating scale? In this case, 1 refers to a child who is easy to smile, interested, and eager to check out new things and 5 refers to a child who is discomforted or upset with new people, places, or things.

4. What would be the rhythm of the drum beat that would mimic your pace or steps as you walk? Would you walk to a reggae beat—slow and steady—or would your walk sound more

> "Do you differ from family members in energy levels, risk-taking desires, or how you approach new people or places?"

like a marching band, readying the team for the big game? Yes, each individual has her own tempo, a desired *activity level* she is born with. What about the tempo of your child? Does she like high-energy activities? If she is asked to sit still, does she get restless? What about talking speed—fast, slow? On a scale of 1 to 5, how quickly (1) or slowly (5) does your child prefer to move?

5. Do you tend to land on a radio station and stay there, or do you switch stations frequently, checking out every possibility? How long is your *attention span?* Though we begin building our skills in focusing attention in infancy, we are born with a tendency to want to focus our attention and persist in something new, or to skip around and change our attention. What about your child? Is she able to focus her attention on a plaything for a length of time or does she move from thing to thing quickly? On a scale 1 to 5, with 1 being that she can stay highly focused while playing and 5 that she constantly moves her focus, where does your child tend to land?

6. If you had a soundtrack playing in the background for your life movie, would it be mostly calm with moments of excitement, or high drama with moments of calm? What is the *intensity level* of your reactions and emotions? Your child was born with a tendency to be intensely emotional when problems arise or may roll with the changes, taking them in stride. On a scale of 1 to 5, with 1 being the most calm and even-keeled and 5 being the most highly sensitive reactions, how would you rate your child on level of intensity?

7. Does a loud rock band get your head bopping or hips swaying, or would you prefer quieter, more peaceful instrumental sounds (or no sound at all)? *Sensory sensitivity* is our biological reaction to sounds, sights, tastes, or touches that are new, different, or abrasive. We are all born with differing levels of sensory sensitivity. How does your child react to loud noises? Does he have sensitivity to scratchy clothing or shrink away quickly from disturbing sights like a struggling or hurt animal? On a scale of 1 to 5, with 1 being the most sensitive to any new sensations and 5 being the least sensitive, how would you rate your child?

After you figured out the ratings for your child on each of the seven temperaments, your challenge is to figure out how each of your child's innate temperaments serve as a strength for her. Identifying how your child's natural tendencies are an asset can alter your perspective, offering patience, reducing conflict, and also creating new ways to celebrate, encourage, and build upon her unique qualities. In other words, if your child is quick to approach strangers or new situations, she'll be ready for developing friendships and healthy risk-taking that's critical to her success. In addition to building on these assets with your child, balance them by offering up cause-and-effect thinking so that she gets in the habit of considering consequences before she quickly chooses actions.

What if your child gets frustrated or irritated with a problem easily? Remember back to our story about Albert Einstein in the introduction, a man who, as a child, was easily frustrated and withdrawn. His parents were convinced that he was highly intelligent and curious. They introduced him to new people and situations that would stimulate his imagination. They cultivated his passions while also training him in managing

> **"Identifying how your child's natural tendencies are an asset can alter your perspective, offering patience, reducing conflict, and also creating new ways to celebrate, encourage, and build upon her unique qualities."**

his anger and acting with kindness so that he could be a loving brother to his sister (which also aided him in self-management skills to persist toward all his goals in life). They cultivated his natural tendencies as assets and offered specific skill-building opportunities in areas he needed extra support.

How can you identify those tendencies in which you are different from your child? Understanding how your child's temperament is different from your own can offer you, as a parent, greater empathy and understanding and give you insight into how to better support him. If he's a little bit country and you're a whole lot of rock and roll, then there are adjustments to be made so that your styles don't cause each other pain on a daily basis. How does this work? Adrien, Jamie, and Michael are a great example.

Adrien and Jamie shared a love of the outdoors. In fact, they met on a hike organized by the city metro parks. In their dating years, they went rock climbing, zip lining, mountain hiking, and cave spelunking. They got a rush from extreme temperatures, daring heights, and first-time thrills. They added travel to their agenda when they got married and expanded their explorations to national parks and global wonders. And then they dove head-first into their biggest adventure yet—having a baby. Giving birth to baby Michael proved to be a first-time thrill of all thrills. Adrien and Jamie defined themselves as strong individuals, able to endure the most physically and emotionally demanding circumstances, so they felt ready for the challenges of parenting. Their new roles as mom and dad rewarded them with the many tests of sleep deprivation and responding to lengthy bouts of crying due to teething or sickness, and they weathered the storm as new parents well.

Michael, as he grew beyond infancy to preschool age, proved to be a sensitive soul. New experiences scared him. It took him months to adjust to the new people and environment of preschool. He would cry during their morning routine as they attempted to get clothing on him. Each article of clothing—pants, socks, shoes—became a struggle. When mom and dad blasted their favorite tunes in the evening, Michael would run from the room crying, hands over his ears. On weekends, Jamie and Adrien would attempt to introduce him to their love of nature.

They'd take him on a hike or lift him onto a canoe only to find him resistant and upset. "I'm not going in the woods," he'd cry. Jamie and Adrien were frequently frustrated and were, ultimately, unsure of what to do.

"Do we have to give up our passion because we have a sensitive child?" they questioned.

They reached a tipping point of frustration and talked it through to figure out what to do about the frequency with which their son was getting upset. And they made some key decisions. They decided to let Michael lead. They would still introduce him to new people, places, and things, but they would do so more on his terms and at his speed. They agreed that they would try this as an experiment. At the next park visit, they asked Michael what he wanted to check out first and followed him. And it worked. Michael became excited at the opportunity to explore on his own terms at his own pace. He felt more in control and lost himself in lifting rocks and discovering the bug world underneath. Jamie and Adrien found themselves becoming more mindful of their surroundings and appreciating the smaller points of interest that Michael would call to their attention. They discovered this new, quieter, slower paced method of adventuring in nature brought them a calm and serenity that they could draw strength from to level their busy lives.

Adrien and Jamie also adjusted their morning routine to acknowledge and become sensitive to Michael's temperaments. They tried on clothing ahead of time and made sure that each article was tested and agreed upon prior to the morning of school, and Michael was far more cooperative as a result.

Best of all, Adrien and Jamie learned more about themselves and how they could balance their needs for novelty and risk with their parenting responsibilities. They would book grandparents to watch Michael for their annual mountain climbing adventure. But, day to day, they didn't have to give up their passions at all. In fact, learning from their son and adjusting themselves just might be their greatest, most thrilling challenge to date.

Nurture Affects a Child's Melodic Theme

If temperaments are nature's biological influence, then there are other, equally influential environmental and cultural influences including birth order, gender, social economic status, culture, race, and our parenting that also contribute to our children's melodic themes. Indeed, there is much more to our child than these reactions, including their growing sense of humor, their playful imagination, their ingenuity and creativity, and their empathy and compassion. These are all areas we'll explore in the ages and stages chapters to come.

In the musical world, if a note is two frequencies higher—and faster—the note two octaves below with a slower vibration can still produce resonance with the other. But it takes sensitivity and intentionality to do so. The same holds true in our parenting. We may begin to realize the discordant notes we hit with our children are often due to a clash in temperaments. But as we learn about each other's tendencies, we can make small adjustments that can send the message to our child that we truly, deeply want to know, understand, and celebrate who they are and how they perceive the world.

Understanding our child's individual temperament helps us hear their consistent, comfortable melody so that, even in the midst of chaotic times, we can respond in ways that show we intimately understand and are working to resonate with their particular sound.

INSTRUMENT LESSONS

METHODS FOR BUILDING SOCIAL AND EMOTIONAL SKILLS AT HOME

"Music is the soul of feelings."
—*Lee Bolman and Terrence Deal, American authors,* Leading with Soul

"I hope you'll become a brave, confident boy, *mi corazón*," Mateo's mom would whisper to him when he was a newborn. And every day of those first months, his mom would tell him the many dreams she had for him. "I hope you are responsible like your Uncle Jose." "I hope you are generous like your father." And "I hope you can play guitar like your cousin Sofia." His mother never stopped hoping for Mateo as he grew, though their lives continued to get busier with two older sisters and a baby brother on the way.

At the age of twelve, Mateo came home visibly upset, clearly feeling neither confident nor brave. "This girl in my class," Mateo told his mom over his after-school snack, "stares and whispers to her friends about me. She's pretty and popular and she must be saying how stupid I am. I never raise my hand in class. Now all of her friends think I'm stupid, too!" Mateo had been struggling to adjust to his middle school and neighborhood since they moved over the summer for his dad's promising new job. Mariachi was the sound of his old city neighborhood, with the Mexican restaurant that catered to tourists an earshot from his doorstep. This suburban neighborhood soundtrack of pop and hip hop felt foreign and cold. "Mama, he's wrong," chimed in his slightly older sister as she breezed through the room. "She likes him."

Mateo's mom then realized her son was gaining an ability to see from others' perspectives, but his newly acquired social awareness paired with his intense feelings of discomfort in his new school setting were contributing to his misinterpretation of his classmates' actions. With this conversation, Mateo's mom made sure she was there to listen each day after school, lending a supportive ear and also questioning his thinking if he was worrying about what others' thought of him. "How do you know that's true?" she wanted to know. They kept exploring that question until he realized he had less to worry about than he thought.

Parents worldwide recognize the need for the development of social and emotional skills for our children's success. Mateo's mom recognized a social and emotional developmental milestone in social awareness and saw he needed extra support. She coached him through his struggles by listening with an open mind and heart. She asked open-ended questions and challenged his thinking to help reframe his perspective when needed, but also showed empathy and compassion. But it all began with her hopes and dreams.

Identifying Your Hopes and Dreams

What are your hopes and dreams for your children? This is the first question I ask every parent with whom I work. Starting with the end in mind, we can better examine how, day-to-day, we can work in small ways to achieve those dreams. When my research partners and I asked nearly one hundred of our colleagues what their hopes and dreams were for their parenting, they told us they hoped their kids would be happy, fulfilled, confident, independent, resilient, empathetic, caring, kind, loving, compassionate, and responsible. Ultimately, this is how these individuals define success in raising their children. If your son's or daughter's teacher came up to you at their high school graduation party and offered you some key words to describe them, what would you be most proud of them saying?

> **"What are your hopes and dreams for your children?"**

In addition, we asked those same individuals what they aspired to for their own roles as parents. Similarly, they said they wanted to be happy, patient, consistent, encouraging, understanding, loving, supportive, nurturing, fun, kind, caring, compassionate, good providers, have high expectations, and be honest. Which of these would make your list? Do you have others you would add?

Exercising Your Emotions

We are all born with the capacity to be loving, kind, and compassionate. But it is our teachers—our parents, coaches, grandparents, and classroom teachers—who influence our ability to act loving, kind, and with compassion day to day.

But how we can we ensure we are exercising confidence, for example? It comes down to our small daily practices—how we model our routines, our responsibilities, and our interactions with others—and how we involve our children in ways that allow them to take responsibility and hone their skills.

My colleagues and I had spent many years helping teachers and administrators in schools cultivate skills that led children to be successful in school and in life. And as we talked to parents and wrestled with our own parenting dilemmas, we were curious how parents' hopes and dreams aligned with social and emotional skills. Because if they aligned even in some ways, there would be a whole wealth of practices educators have learned are effective with children that could be adapted to offer those social and emotional instrument lessons at home.

Most remarkably, we found there was direct alignment between the social and emotional skills scientists study, define, and help schools integrate and those descriptors for parents' hopes and dreams. Take, for example, a parent's hope for a caring, loving, kind, and compassionate child. To bring about that hope, she could invest in developing healthy relationship skills. If a child has regular practice in actively listening to others, in asserting their emotional and physical needs, getting along with a diverse range of personalities, negotiating problems and working through conflicts in constructive ways, and collaborating with others, they develop the tools necessary to act with loving kindness. There are five social and emotional competencies that the Collaborative for Academic, Social and Emotional Learning has defined with a firm foundation of research to back them up that are essential for our children's development. They are: building self-awareness, building self-management, building social awareness, building relationship skills, and building responsible decision-making skills.

> "If emotions are like musical instruments—providing a voice for self-expression—then, there are specific ways to train yourself and your children to use that voice."

Building Self-Awareness

Self-awareness means recognizing and accurately identifying our emotions and interpreting them to inform our choices. For example, if we can identify that we are angry and understand the reasons why we are angry, we can feel more capable of managing our big feelings. Building the skill of self-awareness helps children and the adults who love them to feel happy in life. As adults, we may have been told one or a hundred times "oh, you're fine" when we simply were not fine. The message to bury our feelings may have created a subconscious habit within us, confounding our ability to become self-aware. We may require some deeper reflection to get to the heart of what's really going on inside.

Children are composing the first symphony of their identity, one note at a time, growing in their understanding of their strengths and limitations. As they grow this self-knowledge, they also grow their self-confidence and optimism that they can manage themselves, even when the going gets tough. Our own self-awareness impacts our child's developing self-awareness. Have you ever discovered the disgusted or upset face that has taken you over showing up as a mirror on your child's face? When that happens, if you name that feeling, they'll learn to identify their emotions and better understand themselves too.

> **"How well is your child able to identify and articulate his emotions?"**

Building Self-Management

The next essential skill, self-management, involves managing impulses and emotions and can become the most tested during our roles as parents. Simply through developing and making the mistakes necessary for learning, children can press on our most sensitive nerves, thereby eliciting a wider range of emotions than we have felt in other times, in other ways. How can we manage our big

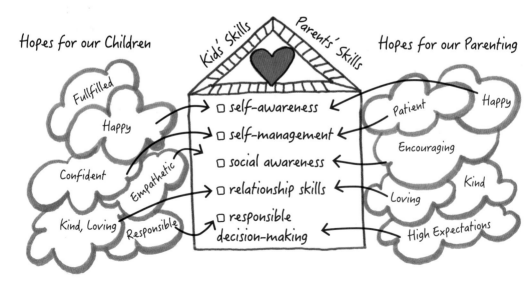

feelings while teaching our children to manage theirs? The ages and stages chapters that follow explain how you can work this critical muscle yourself while at the same time showing your child how to learn it for themselves. Children who are capable of demonstrating confidence, independence, and resilience are children who have

> **"How well is your child able to calm herself down when she's upset?"**

learned to manage their big feelings with emotional intelligence. They can persist toward an important goal, despite frustrating setbacks. And parents who are patient and consistent with their children have also developed strategies for coping with the worries and upsets of being a feeling caregiver so that they, too, can exhibit confident parenting.

Building Social Awareness

Social awareness is another skill our children must develop if they are to develop meaningful, lasting relationships. Parents who help children grow in their social awareness do so by discussing and learning about different cultures, family structures, and belief systems as a range of ways to make meaning of our world. They discuss issues of race and racism, despite their discomfort. They talk about how it might feel to be a minority culture among a majority. They share perspectives on the abundance they have that others do not and how those differences might impact how individuals see the world differently depending on where and how they live. These discussions help build a child's ability to see from another's perspective and think and feel with empathy.

Through the gift of parenting, we have the opportunity to see through the eyes of our child viewing the world from their lens, offering us a unique opportunity to grow our own social awareness. Indeed, as you read this book and

> **"How well can your child see from another's perspective?"**

dive deep into the thoughts and feelings of your children at various ages and stages, you'll extend your sense of empathy and understanding for them. There may be nothing more fundamental to our lives and indeed our happiness than understanding ourselves and others.

Building Relationship Skills

We know that relationship skills are the cornerstone of our children's sense of well-being. If they are to be described as kind, loving, and compassionate, then we know that relationship skills are the ones we must fine-tune. Most schools do not place listening skills on the curriculum, yet consider how they come into play every day. They are necessary for our children's safety in learning rules, for academic success in following the teacher's instructions, and for their happiness in building trusting friendships with others.

"How well is your child able to listen to you or others?"

Our children are keen observers of how we manage our relationships. Do we invest in our friendships? What happens when there's a conflict between parenting partners? Our children watch, learn, and mimic the reactions, responses, and ways we conduct our relationships.

Children also need to learn how to assert their physical and emotional needs without acting out or harming others. This is how they become their boldest, bravest selves—by understanding how they can communicate with others in respectful, constructive ways.

Think back to Mateo's conversation with his mom about the girl who whispered behind his back. The imaginary background singers who might have accompanied that conversation might have sang, "He needs a friend. He needs a friend." His upset may have come more from feelings of loneliness and isolation facing a new school and unfamiliar faces every day. Often, as parents, we have to become sophisticated private investigators of feelings, identifying unmet needs and helping articulate them aloud so that our children grow in their awareness and their ability to communicate. So, too, our needs as a parent can be compromised as we overextend ourselves for our children. So, when and how do we articulate our limits? How do we tell others what our genuine needs are and seek ways to get them met without letting them build to the point of eruption? Chapter 8 provides support to help you answer these challenging questions for yourself.

> "How well is your child able to communicate to you his needs, whether physical or emotional?"

In all relationships, there will be disagreements. Though our children may be tempted to lash out with words or fists when they are upset or not getting their way, they need to learn how to negotiate, compromise, assert needs, empathize, and act compassionately toward others' hurt feelings. These problem-solving skills become ever more important as children grow and the social issues they face become more complex. There is always an opportunity to work through a disagreement in constructive ways, but it takes time, skill, and practice. Considering the fact that most adults struggle to resolve their conflicts without hurting others, it's evident that offering our children practice in collaborative problem-solving can be a key to their happiness.

Building Responsible Decision-making Skills

In addition to developing cognitively, socially, and emotionally, children are also developing ethically. They are gaining a sense of what feels right and wrong. They are moving away from the survival-motivated, self-centered attachment period (up to age 8) in which their necessary focus for decision-making returns to their own needs for a secure attachment to you and other caregivers. They begin to move into the next level of moral development around the ages of 8 to 10, where they can see from another's perspective and more deeply sense injustice, feeling the hurts of others. In this phase, they begin to understand they have a core responsibility to show care.

If our aim is to raise a responsible person and to be honest providers with high expectations as parents, then we need to give our children small and regular opportunities to make authentic choices, to help them think through the consequences of bigger decisions before acting, and to reflect on poor choices to figure out how to make amends and a better next choice. This is the skill of responsible decision-making, and it is vitally important as we prepare our children for discovering their sense of purpose and ability to contribute to the world.

Consider Martin Luther King Jr. and Adolph Hitler. Both used their emotional intelligence to gain influencers and inspire a crowd in service of a vision in divisive times. Both excelled in perspective-taking and communication skills. Without a moral compass to guide actions, some of the skills involved in becoming emotionally intelligent can be weaponized, as history taught us. Adolf Hitler used his skill set to dominate and exclude while Martin Luther King Jr. empowered and emboldened to create positive, inclusive change. That's why offering our children regular opportunities to consider ethical questions, think them through for themselves (with your guided assistance) to determine what is just, and speak with compassion related to others—even, and especially, when it comes to others who challenge us—is critical.

This skill is also a recurring theme for parents. Whether it's wrestling with whether our young child is ready for kindergarten yet or whether our teen should be allowed to go on a weekend outing with friends, we will face hard choices time and again with no clear answers. And we'll need to consult every resource we have—the experts, our gut, our inner voice, our spouse, our bestie, and the wisdom of the ages! While responsible decision-making is a hallmark of parenting and may present a number of challenges, it also presents some of the greatest opportunities for raising a person of character.

As parents, we have the unique opportunity to emerge to the next, final level of moral development—through our roles supporting our children as they learn through the many rehearsals they allow us. We can move toward principled leadership or servant leadership, in which we articulate a vision for our family of how we can serve one another, our community, and the world around us in responsible, growth-filled ways that do no harm. Then, when we face vexing decisions,

> "What opportunities does your child have to rehearse responsible decision-making in your family life?"

we can return to our family purpose and ask, "Will this contribute or take away from that vision?" This collaborative responsibility gives us and our children those vital rehearsals. How can your children make the world a better place? They have that potential, but they'll require responsible decision-making skills.

Voice Lessons: Ways of Teaching Social and Emotional Skills

Take the old saying, "Parents are children's first teachers" and add, "Parents are children's primary social and emo-tional teachers." While we often proceed with our lives unaware of the emotional and social mental note-taking and mimicry our chil-dren are engaged in, the teaching and learning are occurring daily.

Michael set out to teach his son, Sam, to ride a bike. He imagined himself feeling proud the moment his son could ride off independently. So, when he bought Sam his first bike as a kindergartner, he immedi-ately began his daddy-led lessons. He tried telling him what to do. "Okay, push forward with one foot. Sit up straight to balance yourself. Keep trying!" When Sam fell off each time, he got frustrated fast, kicked the bike, and walked off in his irritation. Michael decided to try another tact. "I'll hold you on the bike. I'll guide you. Don't worry." Sam cautiously tried again, without much confidence that he was going to stay up or get anywhere. And he was right. He didn't. Finally, Michael decided to put Sam on his bike with him to get an authentic feel for the sensation of the balance involved. Sam felt excited and energized as he felt the wind through his hair and experienced the joy of riding without the frustrations of falling. He felt safe with his Dad holding him. After several times riding with his Dad, Sam began to initiate grabbing his own bike and attempting to learn how to balance. Michael was there to encourage but not to push. He was cautious because of previous failed attempts and could see his son was now motivated to put in the hard work required to learn this new skill. When Sam soared down the driveway on his own for the first time, both he and his Dad felt a wave of pride and accomplishment. *I did it*, Sam thought. *I did it*, Michael thought.

> "Think of a time when you intentionally tried to teach your child something—anything. Did your child learn what you intended? What teaching methods did you use?"

Often, when trying to teach our children a new skill, it's a matter of trial and error, of figuring out what works and what to leave behind. Research confirms, however, what Michael intuitively discovered—that a trusting relationship is key. Do they trust you to guide them? Do they feel a sense of control? But, the child's feelings around what they're learning matter, too. Are they feeling joyful, excited, and curious? Are they experiencing wonder and awe or obligation and drudgery? These emotions can motivate a child to persist through the time and effort it takes to learn anything new.

Making Music Together

Our children's goal for engaging in any activity is different from our own. Because they are hard-wired to learn from play, magic, and wonder, that's constantly what they are looking for. When approaching any new situation, their question is: "How can I experience fun and deepen my connection with the people I depend on for love and trust?" Parents, on the other hand, become the responsible providers from the moment we see that plus sign on the pregnancy test or get the call that there's a child ready for adoption. When entering any activity with our children, our goal is to keep them safe and help them be successful. Typically, we think, "How can we get this task accomplished quickly before we have to move on to the next thing?" Often, fun is an after-thought.

When stepping back and examining a misbehavior or power struggle, ask yourself, *What skill does my child need to learn to make positive choices?*

When considering how to promote a critical life skill in our child—such as empathy or collaboration or responsible problem-solving—consider a few questions that will open the door to learning connections with your child:

How can our exploration of this skill bring us closer together? If you begin in this way, you will move toward motivating your child.

Take it one step further and ask: *How can this become a joyful experience for both of us?* Or, *How can we engage in discovery and wonder together?* These emotions promote focused attention, a higher-order thinking skill that can lead to flow, or losing track of time because you are so fully involved in what you are doing. Now, that's making music together!

There are five essential ways we can help our children develop the most critical skills that will advance them toward their (and our) hopes and dreams. Let's look at them.

Modeling

Though Michael had a few failed attempts at direct instruction, he found success with involving his son as he modeled riding a bike. But what about emotional skills? How can you model them? If you plan ahead for dealing with your own heated emotions, such as anger or frustration, you are able to model what you hope your child will learn. "Mommy needs a minute to calm down because I'm feeling very angry," mom says, as she plops down on the floor, closes her eyes, and breathes silently until she can reclaim her calm to deal with the situation at hand. This can become powerful modeling for a child learning to deal with her big feelings. Throughout the coming ages and stages chapters, you'll learn how to become intentional about modeling with your child to maximize their skill development through shared experience.

Outside In

"Every function in the child's cultural development appears twice: first, on the social level, and later, on the individual level; first, between people and then inside the child." —*Lev Vygotsky, groundbreaking Russian developmental psychologist, 1978*

Coaching

In addition to modeling, we can offer coaching. The purpose of coaching is to help a child find his own solutions to a problem, recognizing that we are all our own best problem-solvers. The coach—through questions, active listening, and focused reflections—creates the conditions necessary for the child to have his own realizations about his feelings and thoughts and how they inform his behaviors. This deepens his self-awareness. As in modeling, coaching allows a child to feel and experience the skill we are trying to strengthen. Like a sports coach, you allow your child to try out the skill, make mistakes, continue trying, offer encouraging feedback, challenge when needed, and notice effort as small steps are taken. Unlike some sports coaching, however, you never solve a problem for a child or directly tell him what to do, as that takes away valuable practice opportunities. Instead, prompt the child's thinking and support his solutions, as long as they are safe.

Often, for expediency's sake, parents attempt to direct children's behavior. We grab their instrument and play it for them, so to speak, to quickly get through the task at hand, instead of allowing them the time to struggle through it. The essential challenge of using coaching is that effectively playing the role entails suspending our own judgment about the "right solution" to a problem. Attachment to a particular outcome lessens our power. When our child comes to us about a friendship or peer challenge, as Mateo did with his mom in our earlier example, it is an ideal opportunity to offer coaching support. You'll learn about how to use coaching strategies in simple, practical ways in the upcoming ages and stages chapters. For obvious reasons, problems that pose a high safety risk are likely not appropriate for a coaching conversation, since you will desire a particular outcome.

Practicing

Next, we can offer our children practice opportunities with particular skills, such as empathy. We might intentionally create a game when entering a crowded mall, like guessing the thoughts and feelings of people we observe. If we have identified the specific skills we want to work on, practice opportunities can naturally appear throughout our day. When our child comes home from school upset about an interaction ("he told me I was a geek because I enjoyed the book we're reading for class"), you have an empathy practice opportunity at the ready. You might respond with, "What could your classmate have been worried about in that situation? What could he have been thinking about himself to label you like that?" These small, simple practice opportunities can add up over time to build strength in social and emotional skills.

Creating Positive Learning Environments

Becoming intentional about creating a positive learning environment for your children can greatly impact your ability to promote social and emotional skills. You might ask yourself, *Is the physical space chaotic or well-organized? Can my child learn to play a role and take responsibility in organizing, cleaning up, and maintaining our spaces? And what about the emotional space we create? Does it feel safe to my child? Will his upsets or concerns be judged or accepted with compassion?*

Consider the feeling that you get when you walk into your own parents' home. Do you have a sense of safety? Or does it feel unsafe? What contributes to those feelings? Now consider what emotional space you are creating in your own home. The following chapters also offer specific ways you can work on your home environment to ensure that you are able to successfully create the environment of your hopes and dreams.

"How can you create an emotionally safe environment in which all family members feel accepted, valued, and understood?"

Appreciating

When you notice and appreciate the small actions children take to attempt to show responsibility, to try out a new behavior you've encouraged, or to act with kindness, your attention is a source of pride for that child. Its worth is invaluable. When you call out a small attempt at a positive contribution, you reinforce that behavior and encourage more of the same.

Secondly (and less commonly discussed), another tremendous source of pride for a child can be when a parent acknowledges, articulates, or underscores what they themselves are learning from their child. Yes, the best teachers are also avid, humble learners. And there's much our children teach us, including advancing our own social and emotional development—skills that we work on for a lifetime.

In addition to offering coaching while Mateo struggled with his peers at school, Mateo's mom had a realization about herself. "I know, at times, I misinterpret what neighbors are thinking of me. I've been sensitive, too, because we are new to the area. I've been feeling like others are staring at me with disapproving looks. When I started asking Mateo whether the disapproval was really true, I had to ask myself the same question."

Throughout this book, you'll note multiple opportunities for our children to teach us powerful lessons about what it means to be human with a heart and spirit and the sensitivities to go along with it. If we continue to dance in this learning circle, we will empower our children to nurture and exercise skills that will help them achieve any goal they set out for themselves. If we are to harmonize with our family, we need to identify those ways we learn from other family members and call them out in appreciation, acknowledging the ways they contribute to our growth and well-being.

Harmonizing Through Social and Emotional Skill-Building

When parents and children make music together by practicing social and emotional skills, they are deeply engaged in confident parenting. You are able to experience joy and a loving connection while intentionally learning and developing each other's skills. Though this takes forethought and focus, life feels easier as you engage your child's (and your own) motivation to work hard at harmonizing. You find yourself more patient, more understanding, and less likely to nag or worry about controlling your child's behavior. Because you hold such high hopes and dreams for your children, your passions are stirred when they seem to venture away from your goals for them. But when you offer them the chance to venture, to make choices, to manage relationships, to work through problems, then you don't fear their choices or missteps or view them as a sidetrack. Those opportunities *are* the track. It's all part of your dancing in the learning circle and making music together.

> "What have you recently learned about yourself that came from an interaction with your child?"

Learning Together About Development

Families who harmonize, learn together. Particularly beginning around age eight through emerging adulthood, children can learn alongside you about their own development at various ages and stages. This will add to your shared appreciation and understanding of what they are going through.

PART TWO

UNDERSTANDING YOUR CHILD

PLAYING BY AGE AND STAGE

RATTLES AND DRUMS

INFANTS TO 3-YEAR-OLDS

Sweet baby, my baby,
Snuggle close to me.
You're safe in my arms.
Gently rocking with me.
Sweet baby, my baby,
Like the dawning sun.
You bring light to our family,
you bring love to our family.

Snuggle close to me, you're safe with me.
Sweet baby, my baby
How could I love you more?
You give life to me.
You tiny mystery.
Snuggle close forevermore.
Sweet baby, my baby
I'll love you forevermore.

—*Sweet Baby Lullaby*

Our love for our baby can be an overwhelming feeling like no other we've experienced. The wonder of how human life comes into being (and that we had something to do with it) along with the fact that the care for this tiny soul is our responsibility culminates in a rush of monumental awe when they're born. And then, we must leave the safety of the nurturing, supportive hospital to go home where we are on our own and faced with the sole responsibility of keeping this baby alive.

"Jack will start crying and just won't stop," Mia said at a moms' meet-up as babies sat on moms' laps and toddlers wandered from toy to toy. "I rock and swaddle him. Nothing seems to work until he tires out and goes to sleep."

"Yes, Olivia did that too in her first three months," responded another mom, while several others nodded. "It was hard to know what to do."

When new parents are asked what they are challenged by the most, they consistently say that not knowing why their baby is crying or how best to respond is the most difficult. How can you adequately prepare for the physically and emotionally demanding transition of becoming a new parent?

Let's back up a bit to the nine months you had to prepare. As you were baby shopping and being showered with gifts, you may have been inundated with all the "stuff" you supposedly needed to be a good parent. A seat for the bath, a seat for the kitchen, and a swing to switch up the seat. The must-have list grew long as you learned from friend, sister-in-law, and co-worker all the things that could prove useful.

Then, you consulted the baby books so you knew what to expect now and later. Those books gave you guidance on every physical malady—every birthmark, every aberration of breastfeeding, and every spitting, burping, or unmentionable spewing orifice that may or may not plague your baby.

These two sources—the cultural frenzy of baby "stuffs" and the worst-case scenario ailments—can throw even the most level-headed of parents-to-be into a tizzy of the highest order. After all, every new parent is just that—*new*. There's an unknown world to explore, and guidance and support are necessary to learn how to care for the life you've been entrusted. But, interestingly, the greatest challenges in that first year of your baby's life will likely not relate at all to the stuff you've purchased or the diseases for which you've braced yourself. More likely, that first year will be all about the emotional management of day-to-day care-taking—for yourself, your partner, and your baby.

What those books, those baby showers, and those well-intended in-laws don't tell you is the one thing that is the absolute most important to know. Maybe it's not mentioned because it's embarrassingly simple. Or maybe it's not uttered because how it plays out day-to-day can become highly complex. But here's the biggest secret to parenting success for a newborn baby (yes, drum roll, please!): love. This is not a platitude or a pop-up Hallmark card. There is hard science to back up the fact that to maximize our babies' brain development—which, in turn, impacts all aspects of our babies' growth (physical, cognitive, social, and emotional)—and best prepare them for success later in life, babies require our love, beyond anything else on the list. The lullaby that began this chapter illustrates the ongoing tenderness that babies require—your focused attention, your nurturing, and your responsiveness to their needs.

But babies cry—every day. Most babies cry an average of two hours a day. Those who are considered colicky or extra fussy (nearly one-third of babies) cry three hours a day. In studies around the world, babies who are held more consistently by calmer caregivers cry less. In fact, babies "catch" our emotions when we are anxious as readily as an older child or adult might. The added challenge for moms, in particular, is that we release hormones that sensitize us even further to those cries so that our average five-second response rate ensures survival. However, our nerves can quickly fray if we are sleep deprived, feeling isolated, and worrying that we're failing when nothing we try seems to soothe.

The first year of a baby's life is a marathon for a parent—a long, strenuous stretch goal. Marathoners prepare months in advance and, on the day of, they have their pit stops mapped out, their water bottles ready, and their cheerleaders placed strategically along the route to offer much-needed support. We, too, need to plan for our supports. No, you will likely not require an extra baby seat to extend your patience. But you sure could stand to learn some coping strategies, ways to deal with the stress of a crying baby. Planning ahead (at whatever age or stage) can make all the difference to ensure you have the necessary supports to shower your baby with the love they require.

Cry Baby, Cry: Learning a Baby's Language

From a whisper, to a sing-song call, to a stern command, adults enjoy a wide range of communication strategies. Babies have only one most powerful strategy for communicating all their needs and feelings to you—crying. Meanwhile, parents are hard-wired to be highly sensitized to a baby's cries so that we'll come a-running. First, accepting that newborn babies cry every day is important for new parents. You are not failing when your baby cries. Let's repeat that: *You are not failing when your baby cries.* Parents grow to recognize their babies' differing cries—for pain, boredom, or sleep—through experience.

However, most parents also report that they can't figure out why their baby cries at fairly regular intervals. We want to show our love. But incessant crying can work our nerves raw. Here are a few strategies for deciphering cries and sparing your sanity.

> "Babies cry every day... You are not failing when your baby cries."

First, ask what's the need. If your baby is crying, it's time to run through the checklist of what he's trying to communicate to you. Consider the fact that, at times, your baby may have a physical need, such as food or a diaper change. Does he need to move? Get fresh air? Consider that your baby also has social and emotional needs. Does he need to be held or swaddled to feel safer and more secure?

Second, work on your own calm. If you have fed, diapered, swaddled, rocked, and managed to meet every need you can imagine and your baby is still wailing, then what? Keep in mind that your baby's cries may be fueled by your anxiety. Be sure that you take breaks when you need them. Yes, being responsive to crying is important. But if you are losing patience, it's critical to step away. Make sure your baby is in a safe, secure place. You need not leave the room. Work on your mindfulness strategies to help restore your calm.

10 Ways to Soothe a Baby

1. Mimic womb conditions: Offer skin-to-skin contact, hold against chest to hear heartbeat, swaddle (or tightly wrap your baby in a blanket like a burrito with head sticking out), make *shhhh*-ing noises (like bodily noises in the womb), blow fan or hair dryer, turn on white noise machine, breathe deeply and loudly
2. Sing: calmly, slowly (no talent needed)
3. Hold on side or stomach: can help with gas pains if hand is splayed on tummy
4. Rock or rhythmically sway
5. Offer pacifier or finger to suck on
6. Massage: touch stimulates calming brain receptors
7. Talk: babies love the sound of their parents' quiet voices
8. Drive: the rhythm and sounds of driving are calming
9. Bath: warm water can be soothing
10. Distract: examine a new toy or book

Don't switch strategies too quickly. Stay with one or two to give them time to work.

On Being a Newborn

Put yourself into the heart and mind of a baby in utero. Imagine that we are not separate beings but wholly, satisfyingly connected to our mother's body, feeling her warmth and safe-keeping. And, because we are so much a part of our mother, it feels like we are a part of the whole universe. Nothing is separate for a baby in the womb. Then, from the moment the umbilical cord is cut, babies have to begin to understand themselves as a separate entity, feeling completely vulnerable, while still desiring full connection. Unlike many in the animal kingdom who are born with brains fully equipped with the reflexes needed to survive on their own, babies' brains are not pre-programmed, are much more dependent on their caregivers for survival, and have an expansive capacity to learn from lived experience.

10 Ways to Soothe a Nerve-Wracked Parent

1. Baby meditation: Place baby on your chest, ear oriented to hear your heartbeat. Rest your head on the top of baby's head. Slowly smell the baby scent. Hold for a count of four. And then, blow out your air and with it all tension and worries.

2. Parent meditation: Secure baby and then sit, close eyes, and breathe deeply. Picture your breath circling through and reaching every inch of your body. Don't leave your position until your body feels more spacious and lighter.

3. Walk outside: Secure baby in safe location. Walk just outside your door, smell the fresh air, and notice and listen to all of the distinct sounds.

4. Listen to inspirational music on headphones. Focus on the meaning of the lyrics or try to isolate instruments and focus on one at a time.

5. Read a wise passage: You know what readings inspire you. Read one page and reflect on how the lesson might apply to you.

6. Write grateful thoughts: Grab a notebook, piece of paper, or white-board. What are you grateful for at this moment?

7. Connect with a friend: Call and talk, make a plan, or write an email that offers how you are feeling and attempts to make a genuine connection.

8. Get out of the house: Go to the library or a coffee shop with baby. Make a point of showing kindness to strangers.

9. Arrange for your own time: Enlist a partner, grandparent, sitter, or friend. Set up a time (even if short) to leave the house on your own. Go to a bookshop to peruse, savor a coffee, or slowly walk the neighborhood. Do something renewing in your time away.

10. Connect with an animal: Visit your local shelter and pet a sweet kitten or stop by your local pet store and say hello to a puppy. Even brief interactions can fuel you.

Despite the fact that your newborn baby will sleep 16 to 18 hours out of a 24-hour period, babies have the unique ability to learn from their environment, even while they are sleeping. That sleep time also consolidates memories, creating a bank from which they can draw stored information to build upon. Sleep helps babies process what they've learned while they are awake. Researchers suspect that sleep patterns—the quality and quantity of sleep an infant gets—can predict individual differences in cognitive functioning later in life. So, when you witness your baby sleeping, consider that it plays a vital role in her development. Therefore, preserving, protecting, and creating safe conditions for your baby's sleep becomes a high priority for new parents.

The first three months of life are sometimes referred to as the fourth trimester. After nine months, the baby's head has grown too big and has to come out of the womb. But she still needs plenty of time to cocoon—to sleep, grow, and develop. Parents often talk about the "waking up" they notice in their babies' fourth month. As they are able to focus their eye contact on you, parents experience a new level of connection. Babies begin to notice the music beyond themselves. They're ready to grab the rattle and bang the drums. Let's explore how babies come to know and understand you, themselves, and others and how you can best support this learning process.

"How can you create conducive sleeping conditions, including a consistent routine for naps and bedtime to ensure baby gets the sleep needed?"

Learning a First Solo: A Baby's Emerging Self-Awareness

Baby Priya and her mom, Padma, play on the floor together. At four months old, Priya wiggles her toes, finding them absolutely fascinating. Padma pokes at them, names them clearly—"these are your toes"—squeezes them, and giggles. Fingers and toes are endless entertainment for an infant as she first explores how she is physically separate. Next, Padma positions Priya on the floor on her stomach for a short, daily tummy time play session so that she can explore her surroundings from a different perspective while also strengthening her neck, arm, and leg muscles. Padma lays out a padded play mirror, soft blocks, and a board book with images of a variety of people's faces. Though Priya pokes at the mirror, she is more interested in the board book and looking up at her mother to see what she's experiencing. Padma provides a narrative throughout, talking about the facial expressions and what they mean to her. Occasionally, Priya experiments with her own sounds, babbling to join the conversation. Priya gets tired and restless after fifteen minutes and lets her mother know with a few half-hearted cries. Padma picks her up, snuggles her in her arms, kisses the ripples in her neck, tells her how much she is loved, and sings to her before her usual nap time.

> **"Did you know that 90 percent of a child's brain development occurs in the first three years of life?"**

Newborns can only see twelve inches away. Beyond is a blur. Babies begin to see who they are not by looking in the mirror but by looking into your eyes when you get up close to them. You stick out your tongue, and they'll surely follow. They begin to define themselves first by observing, interacting with, and imitating you. That means that your eye contact and close interactions with them are key.

As Priya did, babies learn about who they are physically first by exploring the wiggly parts of their body. And that curiosity for their body continues throughout the toddler and preschool years, extending to curiosity about others' bodies. Beyond physical identity, babies begin to define themselves by the words you repeat to describe them. "Priya is a curious baby." These messages, if repeated, are stored in Priya's mind as "who she is." And, interestingly, if babies and toddlers are described in terms of static traits like pretty, stubborn, or sassy, they will feel that these are always true and largely unchangeable. But if we carefully repeat our descriptors of what our infants are learning and how they are learning—"Priya is finding new challenges. How exciting!"—this feedback helps a young child define herself as growing and changing.

Practicing Is Key: A Baby's Emerging Experimentation

With this emerging identity as a separate being described by Mom, or Dad, babies also begin to understand the world through experimentation. Sand, dirt, and grass go straight into the mouth for a full sensory test, understanding it by its smell, feel, taste, and sound in addition to sight. Your baby scientist might sift the sand through her hands, taste it, or kick it with her feet. These baby scientists make no assumptions about an unfamiliar, curious encounter. They test every substance, observing force and reaction to more deeply define and categorize it. As babies grow into toddlers and into their language skills, they extend this investigation by asking you endless questions that may or may not have clear answers, like, "Why are frogs green?" Parents can build upon this learning by encouraging continued exploration (when it's safe!).

A Baby's Emerging Creativity

We're all born artists. At fifteen months old, babies are ready to begin experimenting with fat crayons, play dough, and finger paints. On warm summer days, paper and paints on the driveway offer toddlers those first art experiences. They will advance from scribbles to winding circles to markings that resemble suns, trees, and bunnies. Offering plenty of interactions with art supplies gives our children's hearts and spirits a channel for healthy vocalization.

Babies are born music makers, too. When music comes on, they will dance, clap, and attempt to sing along. Having no karaoke-gone-bad experiences, they are fully uninhibited and ready to explore sounds. Music is a universal language that babies can voice even before language takes hold. Music offers an infant a connection to rhythm that is comforting and familiar, since their mother's heart kept the beat most of their young lives. Build on this natural voice before language develops by including many opportunities for listening to, moving to, and making music (pots, pans, and spoons make ideal homemade instruments). Deepen your emotional intimacy with your baby by singing him a lullaby at bedtime or when she needs your comfort.

Babies love to learn from stories, too. They're never too young. In fact, there's a version of the Dr. Seuss book *Oh, the Places You'll Go!* specifically intended for babies in utero. Involve her from the start. Can she hold the book or turn pages? Can she pick her favorite? Make story-telling and reading a regular habit. Ask questions and reflect on what you read so that stories become a vehicle for expressing feelings, growing your connection, and empathizing with others.

Tips for Conductors on Encouraging Self-Awareness

If your baby is the one learning the instrument (himself), then consider yourself, the parent, as the conductor helping to teach and direct the use of the instrument. As babies grow into toddlers, walking and talking become important ways in which they demonstrate their independence, but they don't stop there. That new mobility propels them forward. "I do it myself" becomes the theme song of the two- and three-year-old child. Often, they desperately want to do tasks on their own but, with fine and gross motor skills still becoming coordinated, they will indeed struggle. How can you move tasks forward, promote independence, and help your young child manage their frustrations?

Plan for extra time on daily tasks.

Putting on shoes—even if they slip right on—will take longer with a child who is trying to master the skill on her own. Allow her time to struggle through it so that she has the chance to become more adept. Ask, "Do you need help?" Often, she'll want to try it on her own. Manage your own patience by setting your expectations ahead of time. Download a calming app to deep breathe with while she's attempting to put on her shoes, if that might help.

Offer two authentic choices.

Power struggles can become a regular occurrence with a two-year-old who is trying to declare independence. Choices, no matter how mundane to you, offer a sense of agency to a child who has little control. "Do you want the red socks or the pink ones?" It's those simple options that will give her a sense of power.

The Biting, Kicking, or Hitting Drama

Young children can physically lash out at us or a playmate when upset, surprising us with a bite, hit, or kick. After everyone calms down, turn that moment into dramatic play. You might say, "Oh, I feel so angry. If I hit, I might get it out and feel better." Have your child pretend hit you. Play act that you're hurt. "Oh, the pain. It hurts my arm where you hit it, and it hurts my heart. Why are you so mad at me that you wanted to hurt me?" Ask: "Do you feel better because you hit?" Then, talk about the fact that hitting will only make you feel worse. Discuss ways your young child can use his body to feel better, such as hugging a pillow when angry or offering a *pat-pat-pat* on Mom's arm when feeling sorry.

Ask for help.

Twos and threes are eager to demonstrate their new abilities. And helping others places them in a leader role. So instead of entering into an unpleasant game of tug-o-war when a task needs to get accomplished, enlist help. "Do you want to be the leader today and put our coats on their hooks?" Of course, the answer is, "Yes!"

Clearly separate choices, identity, and love.

Young children are not born understanding who they are and what makes them special. And, because their full-time job is learning, they are fumbling, bumbling, and creating messes. Mistakes, though necessary, can place the young child in a position of feeling guilt and shame regularly—depending on our reactions— simply by virtue of the fact that they are deeply engaged in their job. So our top job becomes self-management. How can we create systems to deal with the mess and, particularly, the stress of the mess? When tempted to scold for a mistake, how can you stop, pause, breathe, and wait? How can you reframe your thinking, recognizing this is scientific experimentation at work? How can you ensure that you take the time to clean up together after the mess is made so that your child learns the value of restoring order?

"Accidents Happen" is a *Thomas the Tank Engine* song that my son loved at this age. Yes, they do. But we can always make a good next choice to clean them up. And singing a clean-up song while we are doing it lessens the pain and may even create joy and connection. And at the end of a long day of mess-making, how can we assure our children they are loved no matter what they do or choose? They will only feel secure and confident to explore tomorrow if they know our love is there for them no matter what, forevermore.

Respect the role of sacred things.

As young children form their critical attachment to you, they also attach to objects. There is indeed a genuine psychological connection between individuals and the things they possess. Our stuff gives us a sense of control over our environment, offering us feelings of comfort and safety. Young children experiment with those object relationships. Anything that sparkles, shines, or raises their soft brow is cause for possession. "Mine," you'll hear and, likely more emphatically, "Mine!"

Make sure that you allow your child a few (not a bunch) of sacred objects that are hers and hers alone. When other children come to play, secure those away on a high closet shelf, letting her know that they are being put there for safe-keeping. Then, when you promote turn-taking, those lessons can be learned with more communal objects.

A well-loved stuffed bunny can provide valuable emotional support for a young child while entering a new preschool, enduring a stressful family situation, or just coping with the transitions of the day. Parents can use this transitional object as an extension of their own loving support when they cannot be there to hold their child through a tough time.

Name and accept feelings—especially those of the undesirable variety.
"That's fake," I overheard a mom exclaim to her crying one-year-old at a baby shower. "Oh, that's so fake," agreed another mom. Grandma chimed in too—a family chorus attempting to stop the crying by denying its existence. But there is no such thing as a fake cry. Not really, if you consider that all cries are simply communication. A half-hearted cry might serve as a plea for attention, indicate boredom, or issue a first hunger warning. We may misinterpret that communication, but, nonetheless, the baby is trying to tell us something.

Young children are at the beginning stages of learning about their emotions. The expression "name it to tame it" really works. When your child feels capable of communicating what she is feeling, that very act of seeking understanding serves as a calming force. This is the ideal time to cultivate the habit of naming emotions when you witness your child experiencing them. "You look frustrated. Is that right?" This builds their emotional vocabulary, raising their self-aware-ness so that they are better able to communicate to others. This also aids their self-management skills—our next critical topic.

Synchronizing Rhythms: Sleep, Eat, Play, Love (Rest, Repeat)

Humans are creatures of habit. Even the most spontaneous sort will tend to engage in the same round of activities in the morning and evening. As adults, when someone disrupts our routine, we feel grumpy. Babies and toddlers are no exception. They, too, require consistency and structure. Knowing what comes next—especially as it relates to basic needs, like eating and sleeping—offers security. Yet babies' rhythms are quite different than our own. They require shorter time frames between every need. Attempting to maintain our adult rhythms and routines while also meeting the needs of the rhythms of our baby takes some adjustment and

"Create a plan for getting enough rest to ensure you have the patience to nurture a crying baby."

focus. But those rhythms need to be synchronized to ensure the comfort and safety of each member of your family.

To find a rhythm to your days and discover what works best for your baby, consider two sources of information. First, consult your pediatrician for an update on what research recommends babies require for sleeping and eating by age and stage. With those requirements in mind, monitor your baby to see what seems to agree with her. Grab a notepad and pencil and set aside at least two to three days (to track patterns) to monitor your baby's habits. Record the following information:

- What time does she wake up?
- When does she need to eat and how much?
- How long is she actively awake?
- When does she start to show signs she needs sleep?
- How long does she sleep?

How Much Sleep Do Babies Need?

0 to 3 months: 15 to 17 hours day/night, 8 to 9 at night with regular feedings or wake-ups, 8 during the day

3 to 6 months: 5 consecutive hours at night (considered "sleeping through the night"), 9 to 10 hours at night, 4 to 5 hours during the day (morning nap and afternoon or evening nap)

6 to 9 months: 11 hours through the night with no need for nighttime feedings, 3 to 4 hours during the day (morning nap and afternoon or evening nap)

Guessing games if you are sleep deprived can be frustrating at best. Take the guess work out by writing down patterns and making adjustments as baby grows and develops.

Take heart. Babies will learn to sleep through the night—just not immediately. And in those first three months, some babies may sleep more during the daytime than at night. For your own sanity, be sure that you establish a bedtime routine and an overnight plan. Who will get up with baby? Will you share those times with your partner? Or, if you are breastfeeding at night, how will you get some rest during the daylight hours to compensate? Sleep deprivation whittles away at our self-control and makes our nerves raw. That translates into less patience with a crying baby. Talk over your strategy with your support team. Invest in room-darkening shades or a simple sleep mask so that daytime rest becomes more probable for you.

Love is also a survival essential—specifically, giving it. Make sure your baby has plenty of loving interactions with you and other caregivers during all aspects of her day. For example, during playtime, as Padma did with Priya in our earlier example, consider narrating what you experience when you go on walks together or run errands. This not only enhances babies' language development but also cultivates a trusting connection.

Physical interaction also demonstrates love and cultivates that trusting connection. Recall the power of skin-to-skin contact, syncing up heartbeats when you hold your baby to your chest. Babies cry less and sleep more when they are closely held. And massage, whether it's on baby's shoulders, feet, or hands, helps reduce anxiety while also promoting greater connection. The evidence of affection is powerful. A study followed 500 individuals from infancy into their thirties. Researchers measured the level of affection they received from their parents. Those babies with highly affectionate, attentive mothers consistently grew up to be happier, more resilient, and less anxious adults.

Tips for Conductors on Encouraging Self-Management

Can you recall an experience that quickly moved you from excitement to terror? Perhaps it was when the roller coaster ride thrills became too thrilling or when a horror movie crossed over from entertaining to terrifying? Our young children

Screens

The American Academy of Pediatrics recommends no screens for children under two years of age. For children ages two or three, only one hour is recommended, with parents selecting nourishing content.

have not yet developed their higher-order thinking skills that add rationality to balance out their emotional responses. They draw much more readily from their primal brain—the fight, flight, or freeze zone. Perhaps a duet between the melodramatic Adele and Meatloaf might be the apt soundtrack for them now. Though we may feel they are up and down too often, their experiences are real, relevant, and reasonable, considering their development. So then, how can we help them come to a better understanding of the role of feelings and how to manage them in healthy ways? In short, we can create many small opportunities to practice self-management skills. Check out the following ideas.

Make the mind-body connection.
Pointing out symptoms and connecting them to a feeling word can grow a child's self-management skills as he comes to better understand what's happening inside of him. "I see your eyes are red. Are you feeling tired?" Frequently we, too, as adults, struggle to make the connection between our headache or yucky gut and anxiety. Prepare your young child by noticing and naming physical symptoms and

"Naming emotions and connecting them to symptoms in the body are first building blocks to developing executive function, or higher-order thinking, skills necessary for school readiness."

connecting them with feelings. Post the emotions list on your refrigerator as a ready reminder to use those words to build your child's feelings vocabulary (look for the Feelings Word List in the Appendix).

Practice self-soothing.

When your young child cries loud and long, what can you do? Calming yourself down in those moments is top priority. Consider that those times are your "buy one, get one." In other words, if you react with emotional intelligence, you will not only pass through the tough moment in a healthy way, you'll also model and teach a powerful lesson.

Emotional explosions are never convenient. We're usually facing some kind of time pressure when they happen. And we may feel like screaming, "Stop! We've got to go right now!" Yet, no mom ever felt better after yelling. Ever. In fact, science says that if we yell, those hormones fueling our upset actually increase. We inadvertently make it even more challenging to calm down and manage ourselves constructively.

Instead, we need a plan so that when we've lost our ability to think clearly we still know that we will bring our best to our child. Let's use the ole "stop, drop, and roll" to remember what we need to do:

- **Stop.** When you feel your temper raging, stop in your tracks. Say to yourself out loud "Stop."
- **Drop.** Yes, sit down. Criss cross apple sauce. And if that just won't do, find the nearest chair, bench, or sitting thing and sit in it (ensuring, of course, that your young child is close and safe). For parents of little ones, leaving the room is not an option. Our littles will get scared if we leave, and that will escalate the upset further. So, we have to stay, but that doesn't mean we have to do anything but take care of ourselves and our own calming down.
- **Roll.** Close your eyes. Yes, your child may be raging with angry tears. She'll be okay. Imagine your breath revolving slowly in a giant circle throughout your entire body reaching every toe, every finger, and every hair on your head. Weave a circle of breath around you like a safe and comforting cocoon, and work on lengthening your breath as you go.

We are often under the impression that to show a child love we have to be immediately responsive. Don't fall prey to this myth. Yes, we do need to take care of their needs. But if they are safe and we are upset, it's better to take the time to calm down first than to rush to their aid while we are angry.

After you've calmed down, you'll have the mental resources to consider what's next. You may ask yourself, "What needs are not getting met right now?" Focus on meeting those— whether it's physical (do they need a high protein snack?) or emotional (do they need a hug on a teddy bear or to squeeze some play-dough?) as a next best step. Then, be sure and reflect with your child. "You were feeling angry, weren't you? Was it because you wanted to play longer?" This process is mindfulness at work.

Try other phrases instead of "Use your words."

This phrase has caught on like a bad commercial jingle. We don't like it, yet we use it when we don't know what to say to a child who has become upset. At this point, you realize that this request of a two- or three-year-old child is not developmentally reasonable. They are at the very beginning of developing an emotional vocabulary. Telling them to use words may only serve to escalate and frustrate. Maybe, instead, our child needs to hear, "I'm with you. You're not alone." Or, "I hear you are deeply upset. I want to help you." Or, "Can we go get your bear to help you feel better?" You may not yet understand exactly what the upset is about, but you also know you will never get to the bottom of the problem without calming down first.

Tips for Conductors on Potty Training

The discussion of self-management would not be complete without some potty talk! Moving from a child in diapers to a child using the potty represents a major learning opportunity (and potential challenge) for parents and toddlers alike. Frequently, the pressure is turned on high for parents as preschools require entering three-year-olds to be potty trained. Yet, successful potty training depends upon physical, social, and emotional development, and that learning cannot be forced or sped up. Parents who try may discover an upset toddler and may become frustrated themselves. But potty learning certainly can be supported. Here are ideas to help ease this important transition.

Break down and practice each of the steps.
What steps?, you ask.

1. Well, there's the physical sensation your child needs to recognize. "I feel I need to go!"
2. Then your tyke must stop playing to make his way to the bathroom. That's a big step in itself.
3. Moving to the bathroom might be a chore if you are not at home in your usual surroundings. Find the bathroom.
4. Then, sitting and going can be uncomfortable or boring. Here the child must actually go potty.
5. Cleaning up after going potty can take some physical coordination. Wipe clean.
6. Washing hands should be practiced together each time to prepare him to competently wash hands on his own eventually.
7. Finally, recognizing effort is critical each time he makes an attempt. Celebrate with a song and dance.

Offer lots of practice opportunities.

Put that toddler-size potty to good use. Practice as a game, over and again. Whether your child needs to truly use the restroom or not doesn't matter. Do lots of dry runs in which you are playing and say, "Stop, it's potty time!" Transitions are challenging for toddlers. Taking physical cues ("I feel like I have to go") in the middle of focused play takes experience. And having the discipline (that is, self-management skills) to stop playing and move to the potty is a significant learning step. Treat it as such. Make it an enjoyable, connecting experience. Stock favorite books next to your toddler potty for entertainment. Sit as long as she likes. Keep her company and talk about what a big girl she is going to the potty on her own.

Provide multiple models.

During the time your son learns to use the potty, provide a variety of opportunities for learning—including books, songs, and videos—about going on the potty to reinforce messages. Talk with playgroup friends about their experiences so that your toddler knows he's not alone. His friends are learning to go on the potty!

Engage your child as a teacher.

Enlist a favorite doll or stuffed friend. Have your toddler teach the steps of going potty to that friend after you've had multiple chances to practice through pretend play.

Celebrate small steps with hugs and appreciation (not stickers or M&Ms).

Though potty training can be a challenging learning step, toddlers are motivated by growing big, by showing their competence and autonomy, and by pleasing you. Build on that intrinsic motivation by celebrating their hard work toward a big goal each time they try to go on the potty. Offer hugs, celebratory words, cheers, and songs. Sticker charts or candy rewards move the motivation to an external source and can take away from the values of responsibility and learning. Stick with your attention as the best reward for their positive behaviors.

Create milestone moments when there's readiness.

When you have witnessed plenty of successful experiences with using the potty and feel there's a genuine readiness to let go of the diapers or pull-ups, create a milestone moment. We packaged up my son's diapers and addressed them to his younger cousin as a way to "pass the torch" and let go of the old. Is there a ceremonial way you can usher in this new era of potty use? A ritual can go a long way toward committing exclusively to potty use.

Band Aid: Setting Up for Social Success

Babies are also growing in their social awareness. Newborns in a nursery will begin to cry when they hear the cries of their roommates. And this emotional contagion serves as a foundation for growing empathy.

Consider that a baby's first lesson in getting to know the world is her parents' responsiveness. Is it a trusting place? Because babies are completely dependent upon their caregivers for survival, there are clear messages sent through our responses to their needs. When we soothe them, they begin to learn how to comfort themselves. When we hold them as they cry, they trust that we will be there for them. Building a bank of trusting interactions between the two of you provides a model for your child, demonstrating how healthy relationships work. As she grows and develops, she'll be ready to begin her own healthy friendships because of the example you've provided in these early years.

Cultivating your child's social world—her band—can serve as a cornerstone of her healthy development, giving her practice in relating to peers and adults alike, while also creating a necessary support system for you. Whether it's a library story time or a playdate, bringing together parents and their infants and toddlers for exploration offers numerous social benefits. In social play, young children practice cooperation, negotiation, inclusion, communication, flexibility, and diversity appreciation.

> "Building a bank of trusting interactions between the two of you provides a model for your child, demonstrating how healthy relationships work."

For two- and three-year-olds, pretend play emerges and serves a significant role in a child's sense of well-being. They are able to try out diverse identities.

They can face their most feared obstacles with courage, whether it's confronting monsters or villains, weapons or diseases, and injury or death. Through play, they conquer these and show their resilience.

Playdates can also provide a powerful parent support network. When my son was one, a group of moms formed a regular weekly playdate rotation. Moms enjoyed coffee and conversation while the little ones played. We laughed, empathized, and learned from one another about the differing ways each of us were addressing our challenges. Research confirms this kind of support directly impacts our toddlers' brain development. When toddlers were tested for cognitive advances, the greater development was found in those with moms who had two, three, or four friends they could count on for help. Moms' sense of well-being is not a nice-to-have; it's an essential for child and family success.

Want to work on a particular source of daily power struggles? Perhaps getting into the car seat is a regular fight? Why not use pretend play to turn those times into a positive experience? Initiate a game of teaching your child's favorite stuffed platypus to get into the car and buckle into the car seat safely. Let your child guide you and Mr. Platypus through all of the steps. "What do we do first?" you might ask. Then, talk about what's difficult for her. "Are the straps uncomfortable? Can we loosen them?" How can you use pretend play to proactively set you and your child up for success?

Tips for Conductors on Managing Separation Anxiety

Though you may be moving to the room next door, to your toddler, you might as well be circling the globe. After all, you're no longer in viewable contact. You may begin to notice that, as your child's social awareness increases, so does his social anxiety. Your toddler or preschooler may experience intense separation anxiety, not wanting you to leave them at school. Though it can occur at the beginning of a school year, it may happen at any point and feel "out of the blue." Realize that the anxiety your child feels represents a change in his awareness, sensing his vulnerability when he's away from you. This is normal and healthy. After all, you want your child to feel securely attached to you. But there are steps you can take to help pave the way for his growing confidence as he realizes he can thrive even while you are not by his side.

Be sure that you feel confident with your child care.

Take care of any fears you might have about safe conditions or trusting providers by spending time getting to know the people and environment in which you're placing your child. Do you need to spend time in the daycare center to really know what's going on there? Do it. Take your child along. Conduct a background check, and call references on sitters. If you get a not-so-sure feeling, do more research, consult another parent, or don't use them. Your child will pick up on your confidence or lack thereof with the care provider. You want to feel certain, when your child is crying because you are leaving, that you are leaving them in trusted hands.

Stay with your child in the environment the first time.

Go with your child to the center before she begins, or be with your child the first day and encounter all of the newness of the place together. Point out all of the exciting exploration opportunities. Talk with the care provider and ask questions about routines and opportunities for fun. Ask get-to-know-you questions that will increase your comfort level. Even if your child is engaged in playing, you can bet she is listening and sensing how you feel about this new person.

Give your child a piece of you to keep while you are gone.

Allow your child to have a scarf, blanket, or handkerchief of yours in her pocket—something you've slept with so it smells like you. This will be a big comfort. On days when she misses you, one soft cuddly item from you will help ease her worries or sadness.

Stick to your daily routines and pave the way with happy anticipation.

Your typical morning routine will give a sense of comfort and stability to your child as she gets ready for daycare. On the drive to your care center, talk about all of the fun toys, activities, and kind people who await.

Have a safety plan.

Before you enter a care situation, talk to your child about a safety plan. What does she do if she is scared and you are not there? Coach her to find a caring teacher or mom and ask for help. Practice this!

Remind your child when she will see you next.
Before you leave, whether she is upset or not, let your child know who will be picking her up and when exactly it will be that you will see her again. Use "after lunch" instead of 1 p.m., since she cannot yet understand time.

Leave her in good hands.
If your child cries each day, give her a good hug, kiss, and an "I love you." Then, leave her in the arms of the care provider. Don't linger. The lingering suggests that you might not trust the situation, which may make her more upset. After that, give yourself a break. Take some deep breaths or a walk. It can feel heartbreaking to leave a child crying. Be sure to take care of yourself, too.

Remember it is a milestone to celebrate.
Be sure to tell your child what a big boy he is becoming by trusting that you will return for him. Point out that you have always returned and always will. Allowing him to practice trusting in someone else's care because you have approved it is yet another step in a child's growth and development.

Tips for Conductors on Communication

Imagine yourself lying in a hospital bed. You've been in an accident and temporarily can't speak. As you look around at your family, they are talking about you but not to you. You may feel your frustration and even anger rise if they are coming to inaccurate conclusions about what you need. If they only turned to you and shared their thoughts in a questioning manner, you might feel a little less helpless. You might attempt to make a connection through your body language to help them better understand. Consider this when relating to your baby.

Create an ongoing dialogue about your infant, toddler, and preschooler's feelings and needs.
"You seem warm. Is that right?" Share your interpretations and ask if you are correct. Show that you may not know exactly but are trying to understand.

Teach your baby signs.
Hand signs (sign language) can be learned before words and can lower frustrations, as well as increase your baby's confidence, as he is better able to communicate

with you. Learn together a few everyday basic signs such as "more," "done," and "thank you." These will enhance your ability to understand one another.

Use "parent-ese."

Yes, this is the language we naturally fall into when see an adorable cherub in the lineup at the coffee shop. "Helllloooooo sweetheart!" This language is slow, well-pronounced, and elongated to emphasize the sounds and meanings of words. Research confirms that speaking "parent-ese" not only boosts baby's brain development but also helps parents feel a greater sense of confidence in their roles.

The Birth of a Parent

With the birth of every baby, parents are born too, taking on a new identity with the roles and responsibilities to go with it. This birth is nothing short of life-changing for all involved. Research shows that individuals undergo a major brain reconstruction when they become a parent, confirming the monumental shift we feel take place. As a single or a married person with a career, suite of friends, and a loving partner, you put yourself first and focused your time on your key relationships and how you could excel on your own path. Becoming a parent flipped the script. Now, your baby is in the lead role and you are a supporting actor. Your day-to-day thoughts and concerns fundamentally and seismically shift from yourself to your children—their time, their key relationships, their path on which to excel. This is the unique gift of parenthood. This is how we become authentically empathetic and compassionate. It's also what makes parenting utterly complex and highly emotional.

It's important to realize that becoming a parent initiates a major life transition. And with those changes, we feel a host of emotions that may or may not be accepted in social circles. Of course, we're told that parenting is the most joyful time. We're told "love them every minute because it goes by so fast." But rarely are we told that parenting can feel lonely at times. And the uncertainty and pressure can sometimes overwhelm our attempts at producing joy with baby.

We may be afraid to mourn because somehow it will make our baby feel less loved or reveal the secret that we aren't confident parents from the start. And there are losses we will feel. We'll surely feel the loss of our time with our partner that has been sacred up until now. We'll feel the loss of time to choose what we want to do when we want to do it. And we'll feel the loss of a focus on our career.

Those losses, if shoved far to the back of our hearts, can turn to depression if not allowed to be felt, accepted, and supported as we discover our new way forward.

Like a piece of jazz music, we will feel scattered, chaotic, and discordant as we orient to our new life as a parent. But if we listen deeply, we begin to hear fragments of our own beloved melody begin to unify in a new chord progression that is more complex and satisfyingly beautiful than any we could have ever experienced before this shift. If we allow for those feelings and honestly reflect on them, we evolve into a new groove, shuffle into compassion, and emanate gratitude.

Babies are not born confident. Rather, they are born confident-ready—ready to develop all of the skills they need to become independent. And learning is done best in the arms of love. So, too, parents are not born confident. In fact, if your confidence isn't fully shaken and stirred by your birth into parenthood, you're busy blocking your feelings. The key to emerging as a confident parent—over time, not overnight—is caring for your heart and spirit. Confident parents are also born in the arms of love.

As our babies turn to toddlers who are able to grab our hand and comfort us when we're sad, as our toddlers begin to tell us they love us, we receive their reciprocal love and care and become deeply nourished by it.

"You Only Get What You Give" was a popular '90s song. As parents, we can add the lyric, "You only give what you have." Love and confidence for your baby have to emerge from the care and keeping of your own soul. How can you accept your feelings as reasonable? How can you show yourself compassion by planning for daily renewal to manage the stress? How can you connect with others to feel like you are in this with your support team? And how can you invest in the emotions of your baby and your family so that all feel valued, supported, and loved? Confidence is not born—it's grown. And you're ready to grow it. One baby step at a time.

> "Parents are not born confident. Rather, they are born confident-ready."

5
BASS

4- TO 7-YEAR-OLDS

"No good opera plot can be sensible, for people do not sing when they are feeling sensible." —*W.H. Auden, English-American poet*

"Woah-oh-woah" sang our five-year-old friend like a howling hound dog—sad and soulful—while she was playing. I thought how strange it was that she would pick the somber reflective song from one of her favorite animated movies instead of some of the more upbeat songs. My friend's dad reminded me, "This is how she's feeling." Moving from her current preschool to kindergarten was her impending world change.

For four-, five-, six-, and seven-year-olds, transitions represent a major part of their lives and what they are adapting to. They have to adjust each time they travel from home to school to aftercare and back home each day with different caregivers and rules. And they have to adapt to bigger changes, too, like moving from a half-day play-based curriculum in preschool to a full-day rigorous academic curriculum in kindergarten and first grade. Though you may move swiftly from home to the gym to the office, you have control over that schedule and also have the well-developed cognitive flexibility (a higher-order thinking skill) to make those mental shifts seamlessly. But because your young child is just in the early building stages of those thinking skills, those changes can elicit a range of big feelings, just as major transitions for adults—like moving, changing jobs, or having another baby—can elicit your own big feelings.

The Magic Bass: Attending Your Young Child's Opera

During a weekly playdate, mom Lucy, who was connecting with her close friends, heard a cry at the doll changing table where four girls were hovering. The moms nominated her to check on the situation. As she moved closer, she could see Harper crying while the rest were busy dressing their dolls. She knelt down on Harper's level and asked, "Are you okay?" When Harper responded, her words came tripping out in bits between sobs. Pointing at Mia next to her, she cried, "She hit me"—sob—"and took my doll!" As she was uttering these words, Lucy saw out of her peripheral vision an object fly across the table and heard sobs from yet another. Elise, crying now, too, pointed wordlessly at Mia.

Lucy turned to Mia and, to first check if she was upset, asked, "Are you okay?" Mia seemed perfectly happy playing away with as many dolls as her little hands could grab or throw. "My job is to keep you safe," said Lucy, "and it seems like your hands are not being safe if others are getting hurt. Can you pick two dolls out of those you have so there's plenty for all?"

"No," was Mia's bold reply.

"Hmmm," said Lucy. "Your hands are not acting safely right now if others are upset. Can you think of something nice you can do with your hands?"

"I could pat them and tell them we're friends."

"Yes," Lucy encouraged. "That sounds like a good way to use your hands."

Lucy watched as Mia patted Harper and Elise, who had stopped crying and were watching intently, waiting. The pat seemed to work its magic, and they all went back to busily playing dolls.

This is the opera of the young child. The music can suddenly become highly dramatic. There's much physical movement and expression that goes along with the experience. In fact, our young children are working on their physical awareness before they can understand their emotions. And feelings are at the top of the learning agenda. Some of the big feelings young children experience stem from attempting to learn how to play with peers, as Harper, Mia, and Elise were. Some, as my son's friend was, are challenged by learning the different rules and routines of the variety of care environments. Add to that a frequent challenge that stems from our fast-paced lives and children's focused attention on play and struggle with changing environments and activities (in part, because they are working to grow their cognitive flexibility).

"Through imaginative play, young children develop executive functions, or higher-order thinking skills."

"Time to clean up," you might say. And the response will likely be, "No." Often you are attempting to stop the playing to shift focus while your children's primary goal is play. They intrinsically know that, when playing, they are fully engaged in learning all of the skills they'll need. So, when you pull them away, it's confusing. Why would you remove a musician from the orchestra in the middle of a symphony rehearsal?

We can remember our children's motivation and goals as the ABCs: autonomy, belonging, and competence. Play can help them accomplish all three. Yes, they'll want to accomplish tasks on their own. In doing so, they'll want to show you they are capable. Your noticing, recognizing, or even celebrating those new competencies is high on their own hopes' list. This is because children continue to need an ongoing, trusting, ever-deepening connection with you. That bond is being tested more than ever with daily physical separations from you. They require reassurance that no amount of separation compromises your love for them. And they have a newfound need to belong to a school community, valuing new safe, connected relationships with teachers and peers.

Through imaginative play, young children develop executive functions, or higher-order thinking skills, such as cognitive flexibility (shifting mental focus from one activity to the next), planning, impulse control, working memory, and juggling multiple tasks at once. Whereas in the toddler years, feelings were mere reactions in the moment—impulsive reflexes—by kindergarten, children begin to think before they act. Their feelings begin to be moderated by their past experiences. They can stop and consider—*It didn't go well the last time I took her play dough. Maybe I should ask this time?*—before choosing their behavior. Research confirms that without pretend play, children will not develop these skills that are critical for school readiness. So how can we ensure that our young children are getting the experiences they need to cultivate those vital skills?

The Emergence of the Child's Inner Musical

Dad Mike's inner musical may sound something like:

> *Oh man. Getting Lila into the car seat yesterday felt like torture. Wish I wouldn't have yelled. But it was so frustrating. What am I gonna do? Should I just scrap the car seat? I can't. Oh—I'm terrible for thinking that! Okay, well, do it quick! Wave her favorite monkey around, make crazy monkey noises, and maybe she won't notice me strapping her in. Here goes nothing!*

Yes, our inner musical is otherwise known as self-talk. It's the voice that plays inside our head that processes our choices before we make them. Have you ever heard the saying by parenting author Peggy O'Mara, "The way we talk to our children becomes their inner voice"? There's truth to this in that in our children's early years we serve as their Jiminy Cricket, telling them what's right and wrong. But by the end of kindergarten, our child will cultivate his own inner musical, telling himself what he knows to be right and wrong before he makes a choice.

Tips for Conductors on Developing Self-Control

This is how self-regulation begins. Our young child plays those words you've uttered ("Don't go near the fire. Danger!") in his head as he spies an outdoor bonfire. You may even hear his emerging musical uttered quietly out loud to himself—to control his impulses and make a positive choice. Play assists with this development, as children use their imagination to role play characters such as a firefighter, or they use Lego mini figures to play out story lines that offer them the chance to face complex decisions and scary obstacles, practicing how they can act bravely and wisely. When you hear your child alone uttering the dialogue of each of her small stuffed friends, rest assured this is an invaluable rehearsal to develop self-control, one of the higher-order thinking skills, and grow her first stage of moral development.

Schedule play.

Life is busy. That which doesn't get scheduled, doesn't get done. So, it's time we begin to schedule daily playtime. As children move to full-day school, play in schools becomes a nice-to-have instead of a necessity. That means the responsibility falls on parents to safeguard time for solo and social play. In social play, kids not only rehearse self-control but also practice cooperation, negotiation, inclusion, communication, flexibility, and diversity appreciation. In solo play, children can grow their sense of identity and focused attention and practice perspective-taking abilities as they pretend to be another person.

Create the rule "people before screens" and limit screen time.

Though Micah was knocking at the door, Emily was riveted by her iPad and wasn't interested in playing. That's when her mom, Lucinda, decided to create the rule, "people before screens." Not only does it apply when a friend comes a-knocking, but also at dinnertime, when all screens are turned off and parent phones are put away to fully focus on one another. There is a significant opportunity cost involved with unlimited screen time—that of your child's healthy brain development. Your young child needs a variety of experiences in order to create those vital synaptic connections, and interacting in person with others is one of those essential experiences. So, talk about what she might be missing out on without the limit. Then set a kitchen timer that she can learn to watch so that the "time's up" doesn't have to come from you each time.

Expand the family's feelings vocabulary.

With your infant and toddler, you may have focused on a handful of emotions, such as happy, sad, mad, tired, and hungry. Now that your child is entering the world of school, she needs to become more adept with naming her range of emotions. Because we often would rather talk about thoughts than feelings, we aren't typically in the habit. It requires some intentional effort to insert feeling words into everyday experiences. Use the Feelings Word List in the Appendix (see page 172) as a helpful reminder. When you do, you'll help your child raise his own self-awareness, while also adding to his self-management toolbox as he becomes more skilled at articulating what's going on for him and seeking understanding from others.

Read together daily.

Diving into a story allows you and your child unique access to the inner lives of a diverse range of characters. This experience not only grows her self-awareness as she reflects on her own thoughts and feelings, it grows her empathy and also helps her discover how others navigate complex decisions and face obstacles with courage and skill. Ask good questions and reflect while deepening your connectedness.

Connecting Notes to Discover Their Song

The evolution from impulsive feelings in preschool to thought-infused feelings in kindergarten is a significant development. Parents can assist a child's burgeoning self-awareness by making the explicit connection between an upset and his past experience.

Perhaps six-year-old Marin didn't fear thunderstorms until the power outage when your family had to wait the storm out in a dark basement, listening as fallen tree branches hit the house. Now, even when there's a light rain, Marin hides beneath the furniture, scared to come out. Reflecting with her on that specific experience the first time she realized storms could be scary can help her make a connection and better deal with those feelings in the present. "What scared you about that time when we hid in the basement?" Thinking through the specifics of what scared her can help her make connections to where the fear originated. Then, you can help reframe her perspective by thinking about other experiences with thunderstorms during which she stayed safe. "Remember when it rained all night? We played games and laughed so hard."

"When You Feel So Mad...": Developing Self-Management Skills

"When you feel so mad, take a deep breath and count to four," sings Daniel Tiger and friends on the PBS Kids show, *Daniel Tiger's Neighborhood*. Though your young child may feel mad often, he will not understand how to label what he feels or why his body shows signs of anger. Preschoolers are likely to lose control at school or at home because they are still working on developing basic self-regulation skills.

For the first time, kindergartners and first graders will have to sit down at their desks for extended periods with heightened attention focused on the teacher. They'll be asked to limit their gross motor skills (wide movements) while also engaging in more challenging tasks that require fine motor skills, like writing, drawing, and cutting. Because of their growing awareness of others' opinions, they may try to hold in their upset, and, if they cannot and "lose it" in front of others, they may also feel humiliation, guilt, or shame.

Our children may have numerous needs at the end of a long school day that have gone unmet. They may be hungry, hyperactive (in need of physical exertion), emotionally exhausted (that feelings opera can really take it out of you), or upset by something specific that happened. So, just as with the baby and toddler years, it's important to ask yourself, "What are my child's needs that could be adding to her heightened emotions?" Keeping a high-protein snack (avoid the fast-changing highs and lows of sugary snacks) at the ready (in the car, in your coat pocket—wherever needed!), a favorite comfort item (teddy bear or blanket in the car), and planning for your own patience at that time of day can help. Do you need your own snack and cup of tea for pick-up time? Could you set the radio on the spa station to offer you a reminder to take a few breaths before your beloved but harried child appears?

Tips for Conductors on Teaching Coping Strategies

Though it helps to get your own mindset into a state of calm readiness, you can also prepare your child for the big feelings that you know will come her way so that's she ready with some coping strategies. In fact, if you do, you'll not only reap the benefits at home, but she'll be able to use those strategies at school to add to her ability to focus and learn. Here are some tips.

Practice deep breathing together.

The one coping tool your child can take with him anywhere, anytime that will surely help him manage his big feelings is his paying attention to, lengthening, and deepening his breath. Mindful breathing works with and through the biology of the body. Our healthy nervous systems—like a car, has a gas and a brake system—involve the heart pumping blood and the lungs moving air which are exercised every time we take a breath. Our longer breaths elongate the gas-brake interaction of our nervous systems, automatically slowing down our internal functions and instantly giving us a sense of calm. Three- to 5-year-olds typically breathe 22 to 34 breaths per minute, while 6- to 7-year-olds may breathe 18 to 30 breaths per minute. When you help them count to four on a breath in, and four on a breath out, after a few repetitions their slowed-down breathing will reduce their heart rate by half. How can you practice? The best way is through play.

Try out "stuffy breathing" (or name it your child's favorite friend's name: "Betsy Bear breathing") by laying down next to each other and placing a stuffed friend on your own and your child's tummy. Now slowly give your stuffy a ride up and down as you breath in and out, and your tummy moves up and down. Stuffies don't like going fast, so it has to be a slow, gentle ride. Count to four on each breath in and four on each breath out together, and be sure that you are breathing audibly and exaggeratedly to demonstrate it to your child.

You may also want to try out "ocean wave breathing" while you are playing or settling down at bedtime. Close your eyes and visualize gentle, rhythmic ocean waves on a serene day. Now, to the count of four, breathe in, as the wave recedes, and breathe out to the count of four as the tide comes in to shore while trying to mimic the sound of the waves. You can generate a sound at the back of your throat (also known as *ujjayi* breathing in yoga). This sound will help emphasize the rhythm, assisting your child in breathing along with you.

Talk about how your child can use these techniques at school. If your child likes to play school, how can you pretend play a student with big feelings sitting in a desk? What can she do? In addition, try out some mindful exercises that can be done at a desk that no one else need notice, like slowly touching each pad of your fingers, one by one, on your paper. Do it with all ten fingers while you focus on feeling the sensation, counting, and breathing. Or wiggle your toes one by one in your shoes. This helps your child bring her mind back to her body to care for herself while she is upset.

Create a safe base.

During a playtime, create a safe base together. This is a spot your young child can go to seek comfort and feel better. You may consider ahead of time what few spaces in your house may work and offer a limited choice of spots that are safe and practical for your family. Consider your child's temperament and emotional style when picking a place. Does she need to be closer to you or does she truly want a getaway? If she needs to be close by, consider the shared family spaces that might work for this purpose.

For Gena, her son got more upset if they were in separate rooms so she asked if he'd like a particular corner of the kitchen or the living room. Talk with your child about items that make him feel better. Would a pillow be comforting? What about a favorite book or teddy bear? Maybe Crayons and paper could help assist her in processing her feelings? Or perhaps play dough and a plastic mat could help him sculpt his way to feeling better. Personalize the space with a sign your child makes so that's it all his own. It doesn't have to be big or elaborate, only personal to your child and truly comforting. With siblings, each child can create his own space and respect the spaces of others: Your safe base is yours alone.

Now, play using it. Go through an emotional upheaval. "Pretend that you broke my newly made block tower. My face is growing red. My heart is beating fast. I feel mad. Where can I go to feel better?" Practice moving together to the safe base and try out all of the comfort items you've placed there. Also, be sure to try out your deep breathing practice while you're there. "Remember Betsy Bear breathing? That'll help. Let's do it!"

Don't miss the key by hitting too high of a note with this practice. In other words, if you command, "Go to your safe base!" when your child is upset, then it becomes yours and not his anymore. This removes all opportunity for building self-regulation, since the regulating power now lives in your control. Instead, when your child is angry and you've practiced using your base several times, then offer a gentle reminder. "Would your safe base help you feel better?" If the answer is a curt "No," then it's important to accept that and allow your child to use it when he deems it will help him. That doesn't mean you have to argue with an angry child that refuses to take care of his needs. Shift your focus to reclaiming your own state of calm using the old "stop, drop, and roll" (see page 80). Sit down, close your eyes, and breathe. You don't need to respond until you've regained your own sense of calm.

Read and reflect together about anger.

Children's books offer insight for young children into their own lives through others, including beloved animal characters. Experiencing these characters getting angry offers parents an opportunity to educate their child on how the feeling happens, what body signals may occur, and how they can respond in healthy ways. It also helps normalize the feeling so that your young child does not think she's the only one who feels big emotions. I love *When Sophie Gets Angry—Really, Really Angry* by Molly Bang and *Mouse Was Mad* by Linda Urban.

Tips for Conductors on Dealing with an Angry Child in the Moment

So often, if our child is angry, our emotions become heightened too, whether we become frustrated, get angry ourselves, or feel compassion as we empathize with their upset. Because of our own rising feelings, we will be better prepared to act with emotional intelligence if we have a simple plan in place to deal with those tough moments.

Move to safety or privacy.

Yes, a public location where others are watching can add fuel to a child's flames, as the child is simultaneously angry and embarrassed for losing control. So, guide them to a private place. Be careful not to grab or pick up your child if you are emotional, since your energy will pass straight into their bodies adding more fuel to the upset. Instead, get down on your child's eye level and tell them very simply, "Let's go to the car. It's safe there. Follow me."

Model breathing.

When you get to your safe place, sit nearby and take obvious deep breaths yourself while silent. Your modeling of deep breathing will serve two purposes: calming you down, and showing your child what to do to calm down without issuing a reminder that might be rejected.

Screen Time

The American Academy of Pediatrics recommends no more than one hour of screen time for four- and five-year-olds. For 5- to 18-year-olds, the AAP recommends two hours or less per day of sedentary screen time. Create a Family Media Agreement (see Appendix).

Temporarily distract, then reflect.

You may bring out a picture book, open a calming app, or suggest a walk outside to help change the focus of your child's attention. This can have a helpful calming effect. If you use media such as a television program, make sure it's time-limited (5 to 20 minutes, no longer) and nourishing, age-appropriate content. Then, reflect on what happened and particularly the feelings involved. It may be tempting to skip this if your child calms down and moves on.

Recall that your child is building his feeling's memory bank. This experience is being catalogued in his brain and, because it's infused with emotions, it will be of higher importance than other memories. So, it's worthwhile to take a moment to reflect on the upset. First, ask about what he was feeling. Was it a mash-up of anger, hurt, and frustration? Ask what caused these feelings. We might think we know, but we can be surprised when our child's triggers are not our own. Ask, "What choice did you make? And how could you make things better now?" Following through helps young children understand that there can be different ways of viewing the same situation and always a next opportunity to make a better choice.

Common Pitfalls: Introducing the Villains of the Young Child's Opera

There are four challenges that we may easily stumble into with our young child that can subvert their (and our own) ability to learn, to connect with one another, and develop a sense of confidence. Each of these can emerge as habits that continue to whittle away at our relationship and our child's motivation if we do not become aware of them. As we raise our awareness, we can enlist our inner coach to anticipate the consequences of following these mistaken tendencies and use and promote self-management skills to proactively deal with them.

Meet the Insidious Evil Villain "Rumination"

You may notice your young child circling the worry wagon over and over on challenges she faces at school. "It's too hard," "I can't go back," and "I can't do it," may be some of her expressions of frustration. Our children may begin to feel pressure related to making friends and meeting the teacher's expectations. Listening with empathy for all that is new and challenging can be a real asset to a young child. But when worries spin out into repetitive, defeatist messages—"I hate school!"—they can ultimately subvert a child's endurance. If you have listened but hear repetitive worries, distract. Find an old, familiar toy or game and take solace together in simple joys. Then, after calming down, talk about times she's persisted and stayed strong. These will bolster her feelings of competence as she tackles another day at school.

In addition, spend some time talking about the positive aspects of school. Has she made new friends? Does she like her teacher? Is she learning something interesting? Ruminate a bit on some of the positives of school to change the mindset and help reframe the sense that because it's new it must be bad. If ruminating happens at bedtime, assign a loving stuffed friend to take care of her worries overnight. No amount of worrying will change anything except ruin a good night's sleep. Consider adopting a family gratitude practice like sharing happy or grateful thoughts each evening at bedtime.

Meet the Cunning, Conniving Villain "Projection"

No, we parents are not evil, but the unconscious act of projecting our worries on our child is, since it does not help us or our young child meet our collective hopes and dreams. In the busy-ness of our days, we may swiftly decide that our children's fears are also our own. This false assumption can create new anxieties while masking the core of our child's problem. The best way to stop the evil projection from taking over our interactions with our upset child is a three-step process: stop, ask, and deeply listen. As long as we listen to understand what they are going through, we can feel confident that we are addressing *their* issues and not our own.

Meet the Pop Favorite Villain "Stoicism"

While our son is doubled over crying as a neighbor swipes his favorite scooter and takes off down the driveway, we may tend to think, "Suck it up. Get over it." This is the evil stoicism, a force that has certainly been used on us many times growing up, so we know it by heart. And we may wonder if our "shutting up, shutting down" strategy just might toughen up our little tyke and ready him to deal with a "cruel world." This notion ignores the fact that humans are equipped with emotions to survive and thrive in this very world. Our dismissal of big feelings confuses our young child, sending the message that his feelings don't matter. Since emotions are messages from our core and cannot be separated from our minds and spirits, the child's question that follows is: "Is something essentially wrong with me?"

When pain is blocked, so, too, is joy—and all other feelings for that matter. Though the temptations of Stoicism will be there and exist in all of us, we can use our inner coach to defeat him.

"I know he's genuinely upset. How can I focus only on taking care of his feelings, not on what caused his feelings?" If we distract our stoic voice by prioritizing our child's emotions, we engage our empathy, leading us on the path of emotional intelligence.

Meet the Con-Artist Villain "Perfectionism"

As our young child spills her cereal all over our new rug attempting to pour and be helpful, we may be tempted to grab the box and do it ourselves. When we have the least available time for our work and ourselves, our young children require the most time and patience on each task as they learn new life skills. This is when the con-artist perfectionist can take us over. "Let me just do that," you might think irritably as you have to clean up the mess and move the process along to get young Sophia to school on time. Yet, it's those moments that our child needs to work through—and be allowed the safe space to work through—to get the hang of those tiny but significant life skills like pouring cereal. How can we relinquish our need for neat, organized, and top-quality performances in everyday tasks to allow for learning? And when it comes to drawing a picture or playing on a new soccer team, how can we silence the judger and offer support for the joy in trying? Replace the villain's hat with the teacher hat and recall that each spill, each scribble, and each fall is your young child experimenting with the stuff of life and attempting to gain skills.

Learning the Rules of Harmony

"We have to raise our hand to go to the bathroom," asserted kindergartner Amelia to her friend, Kim, proud she knew what to do when Kim needed to go. Preschoolers and kindergartners in particular are keenly aware of and interested in learning about rules. As a beginning step in moral development, our young children want to figure out how they can act acceptably at home and at school. The rules are a concrete way they can learn what's allowed and what's not. Teachers keep it simple. "Safety first!" might be one important rule. And then, when you encounter a hot stove, you can talk about how that rule applies in that situation. Build on this interest at home by discussing what your basic home rules should be. Be certain to only name three and frame them in the positive—what to do, not what *not* to do. Then you can talk through times when those rules are challenging and how you might support each other.

When your preschooler tattles on her brother, realize that's evidence that your child is working to understand rules. Young children have to look outside of themselves first and enforce rules with others before they can examine their own behavior.

While jumping rope with my best friend, Rachel, when we were little, she once exclaimed to me in a demanding tone, "No, Jenny, we are not doing 'Teddy Bear.' We're doing 'Miss Mary Mack.'" This precious moment was captured on home movie from my own young childhood days for our delighted children to point and laugh at. Back then, that behavior was called "bossy." But now we understand that we were developing our self-management skills, and this was a critical first step. Happily, we remained friends through those many rule-enforcing years! By age five, for the first time, children are able to learn from one instance in which they broke a rule and apply it to other similar situations.

> **"By age five, for the first time, children are able to learn from one instance in which they broke a rule and apply it to other similar situations."**

Tips for Conductors on Consistent, Connecting Daily Routines

Can you picture an opera or musical transitioning from one story-themed song to the next without a transition that has been clearly planned and extensively practiced with the accompanying music to set the mood—assisting in the flow? Daily routines for young children—morning, after school, homework, dinnertime, and bedtime—can offer them a sense of comfort and security. With consistency, there's a distinct tempo for them to follow. They can predict the next activity. How can we prepare our children for the tasks of getting through the morning successfully, taking responsibility for their roles even if they are not yet fully competent?

Routines not only add to a sense of safety but also can be our strongest contribution to their academic learning. Consider that a consistent bedtime routine offers a child a good night's sleep to bolster his self-control the next day. A smooth, connecting morning readies your daughter for focused attention over a chaotic, rushed morning. Here are some tips.

Discuss and have your child write or draw your plan.

Offer your child the chance to practice planning skills, particularly when you're not in the routine. Sit down with markers and poster board. Ask him: "What's the first thing we do in the morning before school?" Follow your child's lead. Keep it simple. Have him write or draw each step of the morning routine so that he owns the plan, not you. For example: 1) Wake up. 2) Get breakfast.

Then talk about the parts of the routine that are challenging, or when you find yourself tempted to nag. ("Get on your shoes, get on your shoes, GET ON YOUR SHOES!") You might ask, "What do you find tough about getting on your shoes?" Together, come to a solution for that problem. Does your child need to practice tying? Does he need a gentle reminder? Agree on a solution, and remember to use it when you are in the routine.

Now, do a practice run. Treat it as an enjoyable game and go through each step. Post your plan near the routine route (say, for example, near the shoe closet) and reference it. To prompt his thinking, ask him, "What comes next?" Be certain to include a loving connection time in your routine, even if it's a simple hug when you wake up.

Use music!

Songs can get a child through a transition with joy. If he likes the song, he'll want to play it over again. Create a playlist with your young child for songs that help you glide through your daily routines. What song will get your child inspired to get dressed? What song will help him put toys away? What song can help get the wiggles out before settling into the homework or bedtime routine? Practice self-regulation with freeze games (musical chairs, anyone?) or singing and then pausing for a number of silent beats.

Reinforce.

Before going into a routine, reinforce the conversation you've had to remind your child of the plan. For example, "We talked about getting on shoes when the timer goes off. Let's help each other remember."

Remind.

In the moment, remind in constructive, calm ways. With any age, parents can fall into their own bad habit of repeating themselves to get a child to complete a task. Unfortunately, it doesn't work. The child becomes accustomed to the 5 to 10 times they are typically told to do something, so who needs to move the first, second, or even third time? He's trained to wait for the volume to rise. Remind once in a highly effective manner, and watch all go more smoothly. It may take a few times to implement the change if it's a change in the child's expectations. Bend down to his level and make eye contact. Give your directions (one time only) such as, "Time to get shoes on." Say it in a calm tone of voice. And then move on with your own preparations, assuming the child will get his goal accomplished. Do not resort to repeating. If it's not happening after you've moved on with your own preparations (be sure to give enough time), then bend down again at eye level and ask, "Do you need help?" Then allot more time if it's needed.

Recognize.

One of the most powerful and easily forgotten tools to use in promoting positive behaviors is to recognize the child's efforts along the way. It need not involve a trophy, a sticker, or a big announcement. Simply say, "I notice you got your shoes on all by yourself. That's really taking responsibility." The young child who is working hard to show competence will feel so proud of this statement. And next time he goes to put on shoes, he'll recall what you said and will be much more likely to repeat the performance. Bravo! Encore!

Favorite Feelings Tools

- Plastic minute timer
- Kitchen timer
- Gentle noise maker: train whistle, chime, maracas
- Play dough or stress balls
- Peace rose, olive branch, or paper crane
- Goodbye hearts (packet of handheld felt hearts from craft store)

The Young Child Libretto: Practice Direct Language

It's likely that your own libretto, as sung by your parents in your early years, included nagging, commanding, and threatening. And, because that's what we've learned, it's easy to repeat those lines with our own children without much thought. For example, you may be tempted to bark, "Jack Johnson, what are you supposed to be doing right now? Get upstairs and brush your teeth. Hurry up, kid. Do you want us to be late? You know where the toothpaste is! Arrrggghhhh!"

Yet a young child requires direct, clean language in a calm tone that focuses on one task and preferably one she can claim as her own. Let's try the ideal young child libretto. Imagining the scenario above, Jack's mom might instead say, "What's next on our routine plan?" Mom waits for a response (mom and son check the poster if he cannot recall). "Great, go for it." And then, "I notice you got your teeth brushed and came downstairs. Excellent."

We want to avoid power struggles as we attempt to promote responsibility and get daily tasks accomplished. We might be tempted to say, "This room is a pigsty. Clean it up!" But we'll have more success with a calm tone and offer two choices that point to the same end: "Do you want help with putting away your books or your Legos?"

As homework becomes a regular part of your evening routine, you might be tempted to say, "Come on. It's time to do your homework. You've got to get it done. Five more minutes and then you've got to work on it." But young children don't yet understand time, so this doesn't set them up for success. Instead, you might say: "When the timer goes off, homework begins."

Similarly, leaving a playground can become a tough time. You might be tempted to say, "We have to leave now. We'll be late for dinner!" Or, "Okay, one last time but then, we have to go!" Instead you may find more success with, "Pick your last activity. What will it be?" Keep directions brief—one action, one time.

Singing the Song of Kindness and Inclusion

As young children's social awareness increases and they begin to play with a variety of peers, they'll notice differences. Some of your young child's observations might make you cringe: "Why is his skin brown?" "Why is she fat?" "Why does he talk slowly?" This is a vital time for parents to introduce young children to race, culture, gender, sexual orientation, learning, and physical ability differences. This will take some thought, intentionality, and a leaning into our own discomfort for the benefit of our child. How can we talk about differing appearances, family structures, and abilities? How can we introduce the fact that some people are treated unfairly? How can we find common ground with others who may look and sound different to our child? How can we teach our child the values of kindness and inclusion?

Take a moment to examine your own approach to others. Do your conversations with your spouse include statements of understanding, compassion, and empathy for those who are different, especially those who challenge you? Whether you believe your child is listening or not, he is internalizing your perceptions and those of your partner. Taking some time to reflect on your own values and how you communicate interpersonal problems among family members can set the tone for how your child deals with the outside world. Put yourself to the test. Notice when you are making judgments about another. Stop yourself and ask instead, "What can I learn from this person who is challenging me?" "How can I find and articulate empathy and compassion?"

Young children, particularly, have a difficult time making distinctions between a person and his actions. A child is tempted to say, "I don't like Billy," when Billy takes her toy. Instead, help her reframe to say, "I don't like that Billy took my toy." Every child makes poor choices, but each child can feel like they still belong in a family, classroom, or friendship circle. "They're learning. We're all learning," is the phrase we adopted whenever our child noted another child making a poor choice.

What does it mean to be a friend? How can the process of growing friendships become a regular topic for conversation to revisit as your child grows? You might consider: "How do you feel when you aren't invited to play?" and, "What are ways in which you can you make new children in your school or neighborhood feel welcome?" When your child comes home from school talking about another child's differences, explore their common ground, too. You might ask, "What does she like to play on the playground?" See if you can identify commonalities even as basic as, "She lives in our neighborhood," or, "She loves dogs, too." Focus on differences, and children will see their separateness. But help children find common ground and they will see how they relate to others who are different from them.

Make a point of noticing kindness, whether it's an act of your own young child or another. "I notice she opened the door for us. How kind!" Use a weekly family dinnertime to discuss what acts of kindness you witnessed other family members enacting throughout that week.

Peaceful Endings

Goodbyes are such sweet sorrow for young children. Sometimes, they're downright painful. Ease the goodbyes by setting expectations—"Pick your last doll to hug." Then, use a transition tool. You could say, "When I blow my train whistle, we'll say our goodbyes and go to the car." You could also use goodbye hearts. Keep a bag of small felt hearts (Valentine's Day sale?) in your bag or back pocket. Offer your young child enough hearts to place in the palms of each person to whom she has to say goodbye. This physical goodbye gives the young child an active role in the transition, gives her a way to show care for those you are with, and avoids hugs and kisses if your child is not comfortable with giving them.

What if she has caused harm, whether through words or actions during play?

"I want to be Darth Vader when I grow up," asserted my preschool son. His hero might have led him to conclude that fighting is how to solve problems. Or his friend's hero, Cinderella, might encourage fleeing when times get tough. Because our young children are in the business of learning and the mistakes that go with it, they'll make messes, cause harm, and hurt others' feelings. We can offer them the necessary tools to repair those hurts through our guidance. Give your family a physical symbol of making peace, whether you introduce a homemade peace rose, an olive branch, or a paper crane. Practice bringing this rose to the person you've harmed. Offering the rose to another says, "Let's work this out" or "How can I make things better?" Smell the rose together. Be sure to model making peace with others. Tell the other person how you feel about your disagreement. Find out how the other feels. How can you agree to make things better together? Model this between parents or older siblings to involve and show your young child how she can repair harm when there are feelings that she's hurt.

Our young child's aria, or solo melody, has much to teach us about our own emotions. Their minds, hearts, and spirits are fresh. They are able to sing free from the emotional quagmire of our years of experience. We can view our shared experiences through their lens, freeing us from assumptions and entering into the vulnerability and sensitivity that can infuse simple, day-to-day living with joy, wonder, and gratitude.

GUITAR

8- TO 12-YEAR-OLDS

"Music is a fantastic peacekeeper of the world, it is integral to harmony, and it is a required fundamental of human emotion." —*Xun Kuang, Chinese Confucian philosopher*

During my son's teacher appreciation luncheon at school, I relished in my once-a-year chance to chaperone recess and watch him in action with his classmates. There were a group of ten fourth-grade boys (eight- and nine-year-olds), who were loudly negotiating what game they were going to play. "Cops and Robbers," said one. "No, we played that yesterday," said another. "Football?" suggested a third. "Nahhh," several shook their heads. "Ball tag!" asserted the first one, volleying back. "Yes," many agreed. I expected to see the group spring into action, grabbing a ball, assigning a tagger, and running. Instead, all ten boys simultaneously plopped down on the asphalt in a highly organized circle. They passed the ball from person to person and chanted...

Tarzan, jungle man,
Swinging from a rubber band.
Pop goes the rubber band.
What color was his blood?

The boy with the ball selected: *Blue.* They continued to pass the ball on each letter of the selected color:

B — L — U — E

"You're it!" One called to the boy who had asserted "E" and wound up with the ball. They all stood and went a-running. No teacher guided this process. And later, when I asked my son, he said one of the boys knew that ditty and taught the others. They'd used it as a way to determine a tagger or a team going first ever since.

Games in which the rules are determined and enforced by kids, not the adults, is a common theme of these years, as play changes from role playing to games of all kinds—from sports to child-invented to board or video games. And, because of this, our kids begin to learn the fine arts of negotiation, conflict management, compromise, and clear communication.

Numerous dramatic changes take place in our children around eight years old and continue through this important developmental time period known to researchers as middle childhood or pre-adolescence and, to the rest of us, as the tween years. Our kids are emerging as guitarists who set their own rules while also attempting to understand a broader view of social issues and where they stand. This is a magical time in which our children are easier to care for, no longer crying (as much), whining (as much), or biting (at all) when they are upset or cannot get their way. They are able to engage in deeper conversations about the world in which we live. We sense they are more competent, capable, and trustworthy, and we can offer them more freedom to run to the park with friends or leave them at home for short periods while we run to the store.

The Rise of the Band: Growing Self- and Social Awareness

Beginning at the age of eight, children have an internal sense of what they know to be right and wrong and no longer need to look to an adult to tell them. Because of this new level of moral thinking, kids are capable of being trusted more on their own—acting in safer, more competent ways. In fact, most tweens tend to spend nearly half (40 percent) of their time playing, hanging out, and interacting with peers. Picture your child joining a Motown band and attempting to learn to stay in step with the syncopated movements and lyrics of his sharply dressed bandmates. The learning they gain from that time is different from time with adults, who typically focus on instruction, whether it's a volleyball team coach, a piano instructor, or a classroom teacher. Adults, when with children, make and enforce the rules. But with friends, our tweens have the chance to establish their own rules for their group and negotiate how they will play together. Group leaders change swiftly as the skills required for each game change. This is important rehearsal time as they prepare for the risks of the teen years and beyond.

Age eight for girls and nine for boys also signifies the beginning of puberty, involving the many physical, mental, and emotional changes that will transform your child into an adolescent with a fully functioning adult body (through age thirteen in girls, age fifteen in boys). Though teens may be able to conceive a baby by the age of thirteen, their brain reconstruction will be in its early stages of shifting from magical thinking to logical reasoning, which takes years of experience and practice to finally establish a stronghold by an individual's mid- to late-twenties.

Parents' roles and relationships with their children will also fundamentally change. But make no mistake, we are sorely needed. Our ability to understand what our children are going through and how we can be a support is critically important today as they attempt to manage the social and academic pressures that increase with their growing competence. As we adjust our relationship, it also lays a foundation of trust for the future that will serve us through the grow-ing-toward-independence, "push-me, pull-you" years of adolescence. Let's unpack how the start of puberty and these important middle childhood years impact your children's big feelings, the way they perceive themselves, their changing relation-ship with you, and how they relate to friends and significant others.

Joining a Motown Band: Children's Changing Identity

For the first time, eight-year-olds define themselves in relationship to others—their peers—known as social comparison. They begin to evaluate themselves in terms of what they are competent in, including physical capacities ("Tim is a strong runner") or cognitive capacities ("Tamara is good at math"). And they also eval-uate themselves as compared to others on degrees of acceptance in family life and in social life. "My parents are proud of me for my schoolwork and my horseback riding." "I have two close friends who like horseback riding, too." This new sense of self that develops serves as a predictor of later success. If our children believe that they are like-able, competent, and cared for by others, they are more likely to grow healthy friendships, make positive choices, and do well in school. Conversely, if they view themselves as being rejected by peers or disapproved of by parents or teachers, children will begin to define themselves as not measuring up, and future choices will align with that view. So how can we, as parents, ensure that our tween's self-image paints the picture of their hopes and dreams—and our own?

Style Matters

Although the clothing the band wears probably warrants careful consideration by each of the members, that's not the kind of "style" we need to discuss. Our parenting style matters to our tween's emerging self-image. In numerous studies, researchers have discovered that one style of parenting promotes children's social and emotional skills: teachable parenting (or in research, it's termed: authoritative). In teachable parenting, parents offer the following supports:

We accept our children for who they are and what they bring to the world (working hard not to project our own worries, desires, or expectations). If our child's interests don't conform with typical gender identities (for example, your daughter wants to learn woodworking or your son wants to learn knitting), we embrace those interests and learn together.

We offer clearly defined limits, gaining input from our children on their goals and how this impacts them. We learn together about the rationale behind why those limits are important. For example, limiting screen time is about prioritizing your time and allowing for a diverse range of experiences. We know there's a brain development cost if we don't. We become informed about safety issues, in particular, so that both we and our children understand why we are making these choices about limits. We focus on true safety issues and attempt not to sweat the details, realizing that our child is still learning and will make mistakes.

We follow through on cause-and-effect thinking and actions. This can be one of the most important yet most challenging and confusing aspects of parenting. This style recognizes that yelling will instill shame and only escalate upset while not allowing for constructive thinking. It also realizes that parent-invented consequences or punishment—whether it's spanking, sending the child to his room, taking away a toy, or "grounding" him—does not teach our children real-world, natural outcomes of their poor choices. It instills guilt and shame but with no clear line of logical thinking from cause ("broke a rule at a friends' house") to effect ("remove a gaming device"). How can a tween possibly figure out a logical connection between the two except that a parent wants to invent a painful outcome?

The problem with that thinking is that it misses the opportunity to seize the real-world, natural outcomes that always exist and hold our child responsible for repairing the harm they have caused, such as rebuilding trust in a broken relationship. We have a chance to use children's toughest mistakes and rule-breaking moments as times to practice consequential thinking and explore ways to take responsibility for behavior and to repair not only broken objects but also hurt feelings.

Let's put this thinking to the test. For example, ten-year-old Clara attends a slumber party at her friend Gia's house along with a handful of friends from school. You go over some house rules you think might be important before dropping her off, including to act safely in her friend's house. You pick her up the next morning and she's all a-glow with stories of laughter, dancing, and fun times. But while waiting with some of the other moms at pick up time the following week, you hear that the girls made a mess during a raucous pillow fight and, in the chaos, broke

Screen Time

- On a given day, tweens may spend 2 to 8 hours with media, with television (including Netflix and YouTube) as the largest portion of their media diet.
- Parents of tweens spend on average nine hours per day on screen media. Modeling matters!
- What kids watch is just as important as how much they watch.
- Get in a habit of reviewing content together before viewing. Check out Common Sense Media for reviews on television, shows, apps, video games, movies, books, and more.
- Watch and reflect on content together.
- Make media a regular part of your family conversation to learn more about news stories that are only watched once and then turned off. Discuss feelings and concerns together. Repeated images of destruction can lead children to wrong conclusions that the incident was bigger or happened more times than in reality.
- Co-create rules on media use by learning facts together first.
- Create a Family Media Agreement together (see Appendix).

a family heirloom: a china serving tray that belonged to Gia's mom. Now you're embarrassed, surprised that you didn't know, angry that your daughter didn't tell you, curious what role your daughter played, and stumped on what to do. How can you figure out how to turn this experience into a teachable one?

You, the Music Producer

Yes, as the parent, you are the music producer of your child's band. You get the cool title but along with that title comes the responsibility of guiding a fledgling band through the processes needed to create a final compilation album all can be proud of. As producer of your daughter's band—we'll call them the Clara

Five— your response to their actions is critical in leading them to success. If the relationships fall apart, the band breaks up, and there will be no album. But if you can coach the band with your child, Clara as the lead, she may have a shot at not only a successful album but also a bright long-term career. And make no mistake, the actions that you and your daughter take will indeed influence the band. So, when it comes to how you parent Clara regarding the broken heirloom, how can you turn this experience into a teachable one?

Feel: Yes, feelings are first. If you are upset, calm down before trying to talk to Clara. Breathe deeply so you can enter the conversation calmly.

Think: What will you say? Have your own next steps at the ready so that you can deal with Clara's upset feelings if she has them when you bring up the incident.

Assess: Begin with Clara the way you began with yourself. Take care of feelings first. It's wise to assume innocence and show care. Don't assume fault or begin by blaming. If you do, she is likely to shut down or get defensive. You're on the same team, and you'll figure this out together. To find out what happened, you might begin, "In thinking about the slumber party, were you okay? I heard there was an accident. Can you tell me about it?" Listen carefully to her story using clarifying—but not "Gotcha!"—kinds of questions that help you both assess the damage. Who got hurt? What got hurt?

Generate: Regardless of who actually did the breaking of the family heirloom, Clara was engaged in the pillow fight just as the rest of the band were, which makes her just as responsible as any other member. Generate ideas together of how to repair harm. You might say, "We know that a china tray was broken. We also know that it was a family heirloom, which means Gia's mom likely had an emotional attachment to that object. How can we mend the relationship with Gia's parents and help repair or replace the physical object that was broken?" Music Producer, this is where you act as coach. Be sure to allow Clara the time and space to come up with her own ideas. She needs the benefit of thinking through what kinds of actions could repair harm.

Plan: When Clara shares ideas of repairing emotional and physical harm, make a plan to execute these ideas, as long as they sound reasonable and safe. Follow her lead on this with your guidance. This step is where you are needed most.

Children will want to hide from the problem and hope it magically disappears over time. Together, make a plan to follow through. What action steps can she take? How and when?

Do: It takes courage to take responsibility by attempting to repair the harm caused. Your support and follow through is essential in this effort. Does she need you to go with her to talk with Gia's parents? Go. She can do the talking but may need you by her side for support.

Reflect: Extend the learning after Clara takes steps to repair harm by simply asking, "How do you feel now? Do you think it worked? What alternative choices could you make at future slumber parties to avoid this problem?"

While this may seem like a long process—and easier to simply take away her iPad—remember that the intent is to teach her. And long-term, how does taking away the iPad lead to this album or career you are striving for—her success in life? This teachable parenting stuff requires thought and intentionality. It requires a little more time, a little more effort on the front end. However, after this experience, which version of Clara will be better prepared to deal with the peer pressure that will surely come in a few years to drink and smoke when you're not with her—the Clara you have led through a responsible decision-making process, thinking through and mending harm she's caused, or the Clara who was angry and confused when you took her iPad away? The first, of course, is about making music together; the latter, about attempting to control behavior (when Clara needs to be the one controlling her own behavior).

Many of us grew up with the authoritarian parenting style—yelling, punishing, controlling, threatening. Because that was our training from early days, it naturally flows from us if we allow it. By using those "power over" strategies, we can expect our children will have challenges in developing social skills and may even socially withdraw. Children of authoritarian parents look to adults to control their behavior and struggle when adults are not directing them. Then, without adults present, they are more likely to make poor choices and take unhealthy risks without authentic practice in responsible decision-making.

The third style that does not teach skills is the "you can go your own way," ignore behavior style, called permissive. Children raised with this permissive style

Facts on Bullying

Our children are likely to encounter bullying, whether as a witness, as a crowd participant, as a perpetrator, or a victim. Because it's concerning, it's helpful to understand the facts and how we can prevent bullying or help our kids know what to do and say if they are faced with an attack.

- Bullying is defined as persistent verbal (most common), physical, or cyber attacks, usually increasing in severity in which one child tries to dominate over another.
- Twenty-eight percent of U.S. children, ages 6 to 12, have experienced bullying, while only 9 percent have experienced cyberbullying.
- Thirty percent admit to bullying others.
- Seventy percent say they have witnessed bullying.
- Fewer than half of those bullied said they would tell a parent.
- Fifty-seven percent of bullying ends when a peer intervenes.
- A child is more likely to bully others if parents are aggressive, use punishment, or emphasize power and domination in family life, or if parents ignore a child's behavior.

also tend to take greater unhealthy risks because of the lack of accountability and guidance. They tend to struggle with anxiety (not understanding where to draw boundary lines) and impulse control. That can also translate into a lack of focus at school. Many of us will have been parented in this style, too. As a result, we may need to unlearn some of what we were brought up with. For more on how to change those patterns, see chapter 8.

What Parents Can Do About Bullying

- Practice social and emotional skills at home and use teachable parenting to share power in family life.
- Cultivate sibling kindness.
- Advocate for only respectful words and actions from other adults toward your child.
- Secure a safety buddy. Formulate a plan with a friend if either sees the other one is being picked on. Practice locking arms and guiding away.
- Coach with simple responses such as, "Stop. You know you're wrong." Practice this and then walk away.
- Tell an adult.
- Unfollow and block a cyber attacker.
- Do NOT encourage your child to fight back with words or actions. This could escalate the conflict and put your child in harm's way.
- For serious threats—weapons, hate, bodily injury—tell school authorities immediately.

Girls Bands, Boy Bands: Changing Peer Relationships

"I had a dream that I told the girl I have a crush on that I liked her and seconds later, the whole world exploded," my ten-year-old told me. The next morning, I noticed him spending time fixing his hair in the mirror, an act that, in the past, may have only occurred once a year for a big occasion like a major holiday. "I feel scared but I can't tell you exactly why," was another reflection he offered. Our eights, nines, tens, and elevens are likely to be spending far more time with their own gender (unless playing with a more diverse group in a neighborhood). They may talk about "the other" like a virus they want to steer clear of or with a distant, admiring awe. They are beginning to notice and become attracted to others.

Our tweens are gaining a new social awareness. They now have the ability to see from another's perspective—or at least try. But since we are not born mind-readers, it takes a whole lot of practice to develop the skill of empathy, of truly understanding others' thoughts and feelings. As a child's social awareness increases, so, too, does her social anxiety. That happens for several reasons. Our tweens will experience:

- Added sensitivity as empathy is practiced and learned. She may misinterpret a sideways glance from a popular girl as judgment of her so-not-cool outfit when the popular girl is merely in a bad mood.
- The elevated importance of peers' opinions as children spend more of their time with their friends. Acceptance now is their criteria for their self-image, so establishing a sense of belonging is an urgent, pressing concern. To feel a sense of well-being, one good friend is all a child needs.
- The changing roles of peers. Not only are they playmates, they are teachers: the keepers of relevant cultural and social knowledge required to be successful. You don't know what music is cool to listen to but surely your child's friends do.
- Mood swings characteristic of a rapidly changing body and brain and feelings of vulnerability to go with those changes. Our tweens are not comfortable in their own skin yet as they are undergoing these major changes.

As our children are pulled toward their friends, and we allow them more freedom to roam, they are excited to assert their independence. This incites changes in our relationship. One day, around the age of eight, I started getting the "stink eye" from my child and began uttering to myself the following chant, "It's not personal. It's development." Yes, this is the mantra that will get us through the intense looks of disapproval and disgust. That is how our children deal with the conflicting emotions they feel to separate from us and show their independence.

Elvis and His Microphone: Asserting Independence and Dependence

Picture Elvis performing "All Shook Up." If you can get past his gyrations and only examine what he does with his microphone, we may just empathize. He throws it out and grabs it back, every move filled with grand passion. This is what our children tend to do. They issue the stink eye, run away from us, play it cool

with their friends, and then run back just as quickly into our arms and may even exhibit some evidence of their younger years. They may whine, cry, or even talk "baby talk." They may relish in toys and interests that have long been put away. Oh, don't mention it to any of their friends. No, no. This is not a source of pride, but a source of comfort. Change is upon them. And they are feeling highly sensitive. Your attunement to their intense vulnerability as they take two steps forward and two steps back can support them through these changes. But you will have to exercise patience. Realize this is all part of being a tween parent, as they adjust to the strange and confusing world of being in-between childhood and adolescence.

From Rock to Tibetan Meditation Music: Promoting Healthy Coping Strategies

Elvis is certainly not our best model for thinking about how we can teach our children the coping skills they will require to deal with their increasing academic and social pressures. However, someone like Viktor Frankl is. The author of one of the most inspirational books of the twentieth century, *Man's Search for Meaning*, Frankl studied psychiatry and neurology in Vienna, Austria, focusing on the issues of suicide and depression. The program that he designed in his late twenties while working with severely depressed high school students eliminated suicide with these high-risk youth.

In 1942, when Frankl was 37, he was arrested, as were his wife, parents, and brother, and they were taken to four different Nazi concentration camps, including Auschwitz. While in the camps, despite being tortured and enduring the deaths of his wife and parents, he was able to save numerous others' lives and spirits through his teachings.

"Everything can be taken from a man but one thing: the last of human freedoms—to choose one's attitude in any given set of circumstances, to choose one's way," he wrote.

He taught others that they could escape any physical imprisonment by investing in their spiritual self, reframing their perspectives. He encouraged fellow prisoners to focus on loved ones—living or dead—who they would never want to disappoint. "How could I be my best self for Grandpa Smith?" He taught trauma sufferers how to make meaning out of their suffering. "What can we learn? How can it serve others? How can we influence the world through those lessons?" There may be no more powerful inspiration than an individual who is able to survive while serving others in what most would consider unbearable conditions.

Tips for Conductors on Changing Ourselves

These extreme circumstances and Frankl's teachings on how to cope with them offer guidance for us as parents as we look to promote our tweens' resilience in the face of mounting stress at home, school, and in extracurriculars. Frankl would offer us the wisdom: "When we are no longer able to a change a situation—we are challenged to change ourselves." With those words in mind, here are some ideas.

Imagine your best self.
For the first time, your tween will be involved in the imagining of her ideal self, and she will use that as a measure for who she is today. How can you talk about her ideal self, and how those

> "When we are no longer able to a change a situation—we are challenged to change ourselves."
> —*Viktor Frankl*

qualities impact today's thoughts and actions? When she pictures her thirty-year-old self, how will she describe her character, her inner resources? How can she show up today as that emerging ideal of her future self?

Make meaning while building empathy.

How can you help your son or daughter reinterpret daily pressures so as to learn from them? For example, your daughter comes home and says, "Sarah was so mean to me today. She gave me a nasty look and avoided me at lunch." You might respond with, "Sounds like she hurt you. Sorry to hear. I wonder how she's hurting that she would act that way. Do you know?" Engage your child's newfound perspective-taking skill and see if you can build in empathy for others, especially those who challenge her. That doesn't mean she has to subject herself to attacks, but she can view her friend differently—with a sense of compassion. Also, because we are all born problem-solvers, we tend to focus on what we have to fix in our lives. Our kids are no different. So then, how can we also ensure that we reflect daily on what we are grateful for? A morning, mealtime, or bedtime gratitude ritual—"What do we feel grateful for today?"—helps generate appreciative thinking.

Use the boomerang rule of reciprocity.

There is a human truth that cuts across all major religions, that of the "golden rule," or "do unto others as you'd do unto yourself." As our children may judge themselves harshly against social ideals, we can support them by helping reframe their self-talk. It's likely your son or daughter is unaware of their ongoing internal dialogue, though they will use it constantly as a way to assess situations and make choices. I caught my son right before he was going to attempt a dice trick saying to himself, "No way I'm ever gonna do this." I responded, "You're right if you tell yourself that before you try. How could you help yourself be successful instead?" Instantly, he understood, saying, "I can do this!" And he successfully rolled a standing tower of dice from a cup. Yes, we need to do unto others with kindness, respect, and responsibility. But how we treat and talk about ourselves is equally important. Use the boomerang rule of reciprocity: Kind to others, kind to self. We all need gentle reminders. You can serve that vital role for your child and offer invaluable training to reset how your child views himself—as capable, competent, and confident.

Voice the whispering angel and devil.

Remember those cartoons where the angel was on one shoulder, the devil on the other? It's time to build on your child's emerging sense of justice and awareness of his self-talk to make judgments. Utter your own inner thinking aloud when you are trying to make a responsible decision. For example, while driving, you might reflect, "Hmmm. I can pull out into traffic fast. We've been waiting awhile. But is it worth the risk to pull out now? It's really not. We can wait a little longer."

Unbox emotional honesty.

If we hope our child will share with us all the ups and downs of their roller coaster ride, we'll need to be honest and vulnerable with them about the ups and downs of parenting, careers, and other complexities in our own lives. "I'm fine," I say far too often, even when I know there's is no authenticity to that statement. And we can't always deep dive into our feelings. But if we create a regular time for reflection—dinner or bedtime, perhaps?—and we share honestly our ups and downs within the frame of a grateful life, we are more likely to gain entry into the inner world of our child. They will not only become more adept at sharing their feelings but also feel the safety and intimacy that comes with honest dialogue.

Discover renewable energy sources.

If we as adults struggle to renew our own minds, hearts, and spirits in the stress of everyday living, how will our own children discover their best renewable energy sources? Maybe the best way is through experimentation (play!). When stress creeps into after-school time, try out a bike ride or a walk through the park together and reflect on how you feel afterward. Suggest a few books that might offer wisdom or

> **"If we as adults struggle to renew our own minds, hearts, and spirits in the stress of everyday living, how will our own children discover their best renewable energy sources?"**

escape. Turn up the tunes or paint with music. Create a running list of activities that feel renewing. Notice what your child seems to be refreshed by and then articulate it so that it can be used anytime she needs it.

Laugh.

Find ways to laugh. Play a family game where goofiness is encouraged. We like Hedbanz. If your tween gets tickled by the crazy things cats do, watch YouTube videos together. If your son loves a good joke book like mine does, keep it at the ready. Laughter really is the best medicine. We can take our lives so seriously. Laughter reduces stress hormones, boosts immunity to infections, and triggers those feel-good hormones to increase a sense of well-being. Plus, it connects us to one another. Good stuff!

> "Laughter reduces stress hormones, boosts immunity to infections, and triggers feel-good hormones."

Break for your brain.

Though we may be tempted to tell our child to stick it out, keep going, or press through, that may not ultimately result in hoped-for hard work. Short breaks help a person's brain refresh and process. Staring at the page may not produce any new thinking in your child. In fact, staying there when irritated decreases motivation to put in the hard work necessary to get through the learning process. But if she walks away, gets some fresh air, or moves a bit, she might feel differently. Does she need a drink of water or to listen to a favorite song? This small change of scenery can boost thinking skills in powerful ways. Your tween will become a better problem-solver when she returns. Being removed from the work setting might even offer her new solutions to her problem. Put that kitchen timer to good use. Work for twenty minutes and then take five and return refreshed.

The Power of Bands Who Learn to Harmonize: The Importance of Collaboration

"Bands who play together, stay together," may just be the next phrase du jour. What does that mean? Whether we are considering their capacity to perform academically, develop strong friendships, or contribute to family life, or we're thinking of their future in a workforce that requires collaboration, our tweens need experience working cooperatively with one another.

Consider the following question: How frequently does your child participate in competitions? From blue ribbon science fairs to sports teams to spelling bees to siblings fighting over bathroom time, if you add up the many experiences children have, you might discover competition as a mainstay. Now consider: How often does your child participate in collaboration? Does your family ever work as a team on a house clean-up project? Or do children play cooperative games in gym class? Do they get the chance to participate on an academic team in which each member has a defined role to contribute and in which the outcome and any rewards associated are shared?

Tips for Conductors on Practicing Collaboration

Despite the fact that collaboration is an essential skill for the sustainability of healthy relationships, whether it's in family life, the school setting, or the workplace, our children seem to get few opportunities to develop this essential life skill. Because the many varied opportunities to practice competition can work in direct opposition to learning collaboration skills, we need to make a point of it. And it will work to our direct benefit as we see family members working together in more cooperative ways. So how? It need not be difficult. Check out these ideas.

Argue to learn instead of to win.
Sometimes all we need do is set the stage for collaboration. If we articulate a goal—"We need to work together to figure this out"—the participants will get busy on collaborative problem-solving. However, if we set the goal as competition—"Whoever gets there first, wins"—any shared insights will not be considered by others. Why? Because when we argue to win, we hold fast to our single view.

Ours becomes the "right" opinion, and to protect it, we shut down our ability to take in any new information. But if we argue to learn—in other words, offer opinions and then ask for others' insights—we listen because we know we could improve our thinking or our problem-solving. At dinner, as you discuss social issues that concern your family, how can you frame it in terms of collaboration? "I have to do a paper on homelessness for language arts class," my son said. Framing as a family opportunity to collaboratively learn, his dad asked, "What do we each know about the problem of homelessness?" From there, we shared our varied experiences.

Problem-solve together on issues of family concern.
Do you give to charities? This is the perfect age to involve your child in thinking through what social issues your family wants to address together. Do you want to improve a part of your home? Meet as a family, and gather ideas for ways to work on that project. Deciding on a location for a vacation? Find ways to engage children in family decision-making to support their ownership and responsibility in your family life.

Involve each member in contributing to the household.
Because of your tween's sense of fairness, she will relate to the equity of all contributing to your household if you approach the conversation that way. How's Mom pitching in? What about Dad? If her brother vacuums weekly, can she take responsibility for washing dishes? As your child grows, it's important that she increase her responsibility in caring for your home life, just as she has growing responsibilities in her school life.

Agree to what it means to fight fairly.

Families fight. That's not a weakness but rather a reality of human beings living together. In fact, John Gottman, expert on marriages, studied why couples get divorced. He found that the frequency of fighting didn't matter when it came to couples who stayed together versus those that did not. All fought. The difference was in *how* they fought.

One of the factors he discovered in successful long-term relationships was that healthy couples balanced their negativity with positivity. There was, in fact, a magical amount of five positive interactions to one negative interaction, called the Gottman Ratio, that allowed for sustainable relationships. This is true with our parent-child and sibling relationships as well. Consider a particularly difficult day with your kids. Did they have five positive interactions with you to counteract the one challenging one?

Consider that the way we talk to our partner becomes the way that our child speaks to them, too. I noticed that my son started thanking me for dinner after my husband thanked me a number of times. How do we appreciate the work that our partner puts into our life? Yes, we may put in hard work, too, maybe even the lion's share. But recognizing and appreciating even small contributions creates a culture of appreciation in family life that translates into appreciative children.

Studies show that kids who lived in households with regular parental fighting experienced a higher stress level than others who lived in more peaceful households. Over time, that stress compromised the children's brain development, leading to impairments in learning and memory. But kids who lived in households in which parents argued but genuinely resolved the arguments (kids were aware if parents faked a resolution) were actually happier than before they experienced the argument. Why? Because they learned that their parents can fight and work it out. Their family survival was not at risk every time there was an argument. The Families Fighting Fairly Pledge in the Appendix (see page 174) is a useful tool to help your family argue constructively.

As we examine the ways that develop or destroy our relationships when disagreeing, it's evident that how we use and share power matters greatly when it comes to family members feeling accepted, valued, and empowered to be their best selves.

The Star Qualities of Our Band Members

It's no accident that some of the most beloved children's characters in movies and books—*Harry Potter* and *Anne of Green Gables,* to name a few—are depicted at this tween age. It's a magical time in which children are capable of sophisticated questions and thinking about the larger world as they broaden their circle of concern. Yet, they remain deeply connected to and dependent on our daily family life. They are no longer merely cared for but become capable givers of care. We can deepen our own empathy skills as we offer our children authentic practice for their growing social awareness.

• How can we learn from others together, especially those who challenge us?

• How can we support our children in acting with compassion?

• And how can we expand our own circle of concern by exercising compassion with them?

We have the opportunity right now to deepen our intimacy and trust with our children as they explore new worlds, discover a sense of meaning in their relationships, and reach out to others to make their lives better—if only we act together. When we do, we set the stage for our children's bright, long-term career of healthy, fulfilling relationships with friends, with us, and with themselves.

HORNS

13- TO 17-YEAR-OLDS

"Music is your own experience, your own thoughts, your wisdom. If you don't
live it, it won't come out of your horn."
—*Charlie Parker, American jazz saxophonist and composer*

"Erika spends most of her time after school in her room," my client, Anna, mother of thirteen-year-old Erika, said with a sad tone in her voice. "I knock and offer her a snack but she responds with one word: No." Anna relayed that Erika would spend hours in her room on her laptop and worried she was up to something. But what? Erika also seemed highly sensitive when Anna insinuated Erika (formerly a straight "A" student) or her friends might not be living up to their potential. Erika seemed to have lost much of her motivation for working hard, particularly on longer-term projects. The discordant notes shared between Erika and her mom had become frequent, distancing, and uncomfortable.

"But then, when I'm making dinner some days, she'll just lean her head on my shoulder. She's reaching out. But I don't know what to say. She can be so moody, even rude, and then she wants to connect. I feel like I'm walking on eggshells. It's confusing, to say the least."

Though teens have the musical skill and understanding of each age and stage behind them, they face new learning challenges in this unique time of life. Because they are in the process of reforming who they are and who they want to be, they may create a wide range of sounds that can sway with unpredictably, from the pout of the tuba to the excitement of a trumpet to the whine of the clarinet. They're joining the marching band—attempting to fit into a more expansive teen culture—and, as parents, we have much to learn about how we can support their development and continue to play a key role throughout these critical years of life.

Learning Patience and Understanding

According to recent surveys, the top challenge and priority for parenting was patience and understanding. That ability can become a particular challenge as children move into their teenage years. They are striving for independence yet are still very much dependent on you for your guidance, love, and support. Their bodies are looking taller and more mature, with features that resemble an adult's, but their behaviors do not demonstrate that maturity. That paradox can be confusing for parents—and teens too—as they navigate increasing complexities in school, their friendships, and their involvement in family life.

Parents of teenagers are clear about their challenges. They want to know about digital life, about increasing desires for privacy, about risk-taking and where they should draw firm boundary lines and where they should let go, and also about moodiness—teens pushing them away, asserting independence, and then snapping back, desperately needing them. To expand our patience and understanding for our teenagers, it helps to place our own heads into their emotional world. The teen years can be considered a birth—or perhaps a rebirth. Our children are transforming into adults before our very eyes. As they experiment with new ways of thinking in the adult realm, they also bring the child in them to every moment. Teens exist in the in-between.

There's much we can learn about our teens by reflecting on how we felt after their actual birth. After all, that also marked the birth of our own new identity. Ask yourself: How did I feel in those very first days of being a new parent? I felt scared, overwhelmed, vulnerable, isolated, happy, amazed, in love, ignorant, empathetic, overjoyed, excited, confused, daunted, edgy, sleep-deprived, and sad for the loss of the life before kids. What a mash-up! What feelings might you add to the list?

These are the same emotions that your teenager experiences as she exists in the in-between. Teens are letting go of their childhood while also holding onto it, which can be exciting, thrilling, confusing, sad, anxiety-ridden, and isolating.

"Heart and Soul" Force: Our Teen's Developmental Impulses

Do you remember "Heart and Soul," that piano duet so many learned to play as a first easy piece? Think about the basic melody. It's starts: "Heart and soul (middle C, C, C)." Now stop. If you are humming along, is it easy for you to stop with those first three notes? Or do you feel the urge to hum the next bars? This pull resembles how it feels for our teenagers who have developmental needs urging them on.

Deep down, all children and teenagers know exactly what's next on their learning agenda. This is their built-in GPS (or, IPS: inner positioning system). They are attracted to it. In fact, adults don't lose this IPS. Adults tend to become more adept at ignoring their IPS, but we all have it. Confident teens learn to listen to their IPS and become more skilled at managing and making healthy choices by following their IPS in thoughtful ways.

Teens are capable of placing their IPS urgings on hold. And we, as parents, can require them to by punishing impulsive choices or overprotecting their every move. But that stoppage can create problems. Just as we stuff down our emotions only to have them well up and explode, our teens can stuff down their developmental needs only so long. In fact, teens who are not allowed to pursue their inherent needs can become depressed or anxious.

Teens are not merely going through a major body reconstruction with changes that move them physically from a child to an adult. We have commonly heard the culprit for teen's behavior is their "raging hormones," but this framing paints only a fraction of the full developmental picture. Teens are simultaneously going through a major brain reconstruction. Young children's brains are wired to learn through play (and we never lose that ability), but in the teen years the brain shifts toward the logical reasoning that will be required of their adult years. However, those connections to rational thinking will not be well-established until their mid- to late-twenties. These significant brain changes result in individuals with larger bodies who are more impulsive, easily excitable, and eager for new experiences but less able to make connections between their desires and what might be the outcome of acting upon them. This can add to teens' high level of sensitivity to any judgments made on their ever-evolving, murky identity.

Teens stand at the gateway to adulthood and, upon first glance, the freedom of it all looks magical. They fall in love fast and hard for each other and the ideals and hopes for their future. But they also face the overwhelming sense that they are not knowledgeable about the world or fully ready to be on their own. That magical world is daunting and, at times, dangerous. They are glimpsing an independent future and increasingly realize that their parents have to let go of their arm to allow them their own life forward. It can be a terrifying notion in which they feel completely unprepared.

How do we respond as parents when developmental needs call them to take risks, act impulsively, and conform to their friends' opinions? Let's get into the specifics.

Learning About Our Teen's Developmental Road Map

There are five common elements that help provide a developmental road map for understanding our teen's changes and the emotions that accompany them. Interestingly, all the social and emotional skills we have highlighted up to this point that build up our confident kids at each age and stage directly align with those themes. We'll first identify them and then figure out together how parents can respond in ways that promote skill development and healthy choices.

Voice Lessons: Teen's Emerging Adult Identity

Finding a unique voice is a central vocation of the teen years, with impacts on everything from style and appearance to language, ethics, and passions. Adults have defined your teen's identity so far in his life. "You're a strong athlete," or "You're so stubborn." That has been enough to define him until now. But teenagers must determine their chosen adult identity—one that will stay with them and guide big life-defining choices ahead. Their *self-awareness* is reforming. Will they marry? Will they pursue a passion for a career? Will they adopt a cause? Now, it's your teen's turn to define his identity for himself. Teens look to multiple sources to provide information on how to redefine themselves. They find clues through:

- Experimentation (testing limits, making mistakes)
- Peers' opinions (read: judgments)
- Their own inner voice (both their inner wisdom and their inner doubt, fear, self-loathing)
- Views of authority figures (parents, teachers, coaches, mentors, grandparents)

Collecting data from four differing data sets means a whole lot of information to sort out. It's no wonder that your teen doesn't figure out who he is for quite a while.

Consider a time when your identity felt murky. Go back to the feelings of becoming new parents. Your nerves were probably raw. You felt highly insecure. You could become upset, frustrated, or angry much more quickly because you didn't have your bearings. Everything seemed new and challenging. Parents of teens may notice the same level of sensitivity—and, along with it, an unpredictability as to when a hot button could be pressed.

Tips for Conductors on Supporting Your Teen's Emerging Adult Identity

Considering how we deal with transitions emotionally can help us better understand this heightened sensitivity in our teens. The life stages of a caterpillar transforming into a butterfly are a perfect example. The caterpillar has a fully defined sense of self, green with white stripes, happily munching a leaf. When he's ready, he will weave his own chrysalis (read: your teen's bedroom and the inner private world he creates) where he can be alone during this rocky transition. When he is safely enshrouded in the chrysalis, he turns into "goo." The caterpillar becomes a unique substance for that time of change that he's never been before and will never be again. But this "goo" state is necessary for him to become the butterfly that he knows in his heart he will be. If someone were to come along and remove him from his chrysalis, he would die. That's how vulnerable he is. Though it's terribly uncomfortable to be so defenseless, he knows it's necessary. Great beauty, confidence, and sense of identity await just ahead. But he'll have to manage his own tumultuous feelings in the in-between. Your compassion and understanding of this unique time can go a long way toward

helping your teen feel safe and supported. The following offer specific helpful tips.

Be ready to listen when teens are ready to talk.

Teens may not want to respond to probing questions on the spot. After all, they are trying to assert independence, but haven't truly found it yet. So, look for occasions when you are together, not staring eyeball to eyeball. Go to your son's room, knock first, and hang out in his world for a little while, with your only goal to make a connection. Be there as an open, trusting support and avoid the "Gotcha!" or "I'm listening to catch a fault you made and call you on it." Practice reflective listening. Ask good questions, reflect back his thoughts and feelings, and leave your judgments behind. This openness on your part will build trust so that, when he runs into problems, he will be more likely to come to you.

Normalize talking about feelings.

Because of teens' heightened sensitivity, it helps to make the expression of feelings a regular part of family conversation ("I was nervous today about my meeting, but it all went okay."). Because discussion of emotions seems normal, your son may be more willing to admit to his feelings. And that admission may offer understanding, connection with you, and possibly some relief from the isolation and pressures he might be experiencing.

Respect alone time.

Though you want to connect with your teen, she also requires her privacy to be alone and talk with her friends. Give her time in her room with her door shut. Try not to make assumptions about what's she's doing. She's likely not plotting to run away. She may just be licking her wounds from being ignored by the classmate she likes. Supply books, journals, and drawing pads so that she has the reflective tools needed.

Talk about discovering a unique sense of purpose.

As your teen's new identity forms, she'll benefit from searching for an anchor, a focal point for her life. You can introduce your teen to the search for her sense of purpose with questions such as, "What do you love and lose track of time doing?" and also, "How can you envision a better world and what could you contribute to it?"

Model this by talking about your own sense of purpose. What gives your life meaning? How did you discover your sense of purpose? If you are currently engaged in your own search, share what that feels like and how you are deeply reflecting to uncover it for yourself. This engages your teen in her very own hero's journey, in which she listens deeply to her own inner urgings and feels supported and emboldened to articulate how she could make her mark and contribute to a better world. This not only helps reduce anxiety, offering clarity and focus, but it also allows your

> "Engage your teen in her very own hero's journey, in which she listens deeply to her own inner urgings and feels supported."

teen a new lens through which to view her goals, her education, and ultimately, her identity as one who can envision a life as a contributor to others.

Show your love.
Because our teen's IPS (see page 132) is set to pull away, we may begin to show affection less. After all, our teen seems to require distance. But, make no mistake, they still benefit from your love and may need to hear it more than ever in this time of sensitivity. Find a way to regularly get in a hug or words of support. Your effort to make a point of it could be the loving foundation they require to bolster their resilience.

Shifting Band Leaders: Growing Social Awareness and Anxiety

The leader of the band changes during the teen years. Whereas you were once the producer, now teens take more of their cues on what to say, do, and "like" from their peers. But, despite this shift, you are reading this chapter because you know that your influence remains powerful.

During the teenage brain reconstruction, teens gain the ability to think abstractly. The functions that relate to feeling fear and anxiety, to how teens perceive others, and to *self-control* move from the primitive parts of the brain (the amygdala) to the prefrontal cortex, the front of the brain that develops last and is responsible for logical thinking. During this necessary shift, teens can generate thinking that we, as adults, may question. You may think, "Tom's not mad at you. I'm not sure where you're getting that from?" As the brain strengthens its understanding of ascribing meaning to other's actions and motivations and of linking cause to effect, your teen will require practice in making those connections. This shift is an important part of their development.

Your daughter may share a friend's challenge. "I can't believe Susie lied to her parents about going to that party. I mean, I get why she wanted to go; everyone was there. But she is going to be in so much trouble. I would have just been upfront about it." In this instance, she is matching an action with a consequence (lie = busted), empathizing with Susie's perspective, and considering what she might do given the same circumstances. Could your nine-year-old make all of those leaps in thinking? Not a chance.

There's a cost to this maturation in thinking. It might be akin to getting glasses after not being able to see very well. The clarity is shocking at first. It may make a person feel disoriented but also overjoyed by his newfound sight. And, if you can see flaws on your face that weren't apparent to you before, certainly you'll be more self-conscious now that you've spotted them.

As teens begin to see others' perspectives, this can cause intense anxiety. Disapproval from or a lack of connection with peers can cause fear for their very survival. After all, they know those social connections will become their central relationships once they have left the safety of your home. To add to this feeling of insecurity, their self-image is cocooning, vulnerable, and unsure. Each peer that passes by offering a glare (that may, in fact, have nothing to do them) could send a teen into a swirling vortex of predictions about the other person's thoughts and feelings (*Did he notice my new jeans? I'll bet he thought they were ugly.*). Teens may feel like they are constantly in the spotlight being evaluated as they exercise their fledgling empathy.

Tips for Conductors on Managing Anxiety

With a teen's growing social awareness, she'll have to learn to manage the anxiety that grows right along with it. Your support can become invaluable. Though the power of their peers' words, glares, and stares may sting, you can help them gain a larger perspective.

Practice coping strategies.

Did you know that an estimated one-third of teens experience a high level of ongoing anxiety? Share with your teen that you, too, feel anxiety. Take some deep breaths. Sit down to calm down when needed. Take walks or hikes to spend time in nature. Modeling ways you take care of yourself when you feel anxious will help your teen develop her own strategies.

Guide with healthy ways to deal with big feelings.

Anxiety often pairs with other emotions that teens may not know how to handle, such as anger, frustration, or hurt from feeling judged by peers. How can a teen deal with the strong feelings that arise from rejection? Your modeling will be their first guide. But also, let them know that expressing anger can be important and healthy, but only in ways that expel the fire of it. For example, screaming or yelling only increases the fight-or-flight hormones and fuels the flames further. Instead, you may talk together about what kinds of actions help your teen feel calmer. Does a walk while listening to music help? Can she close her eyes and visualize herself on her favorite beach? Check out the Emotional Safety Plan in the Appendix to help your teen plan for her intense moments.

Express curiosity about friends but not judgment.

Friendships change rapidly in the teen's world, and there's no way an adult can keep up. Instead of trying, ask good open-ended questions and express concern and curiosity without criticizing. Give teens the benefit of the doubt, just as you might with your own long-term friendships. Your daughter might be more willing to come to you with worries if you offer support and accept her friends as her own to manage.

Practice reframing and viewing alternative perspectives.

Since your teen is practicing her new empathy skill set, why not consider offering up alternative interpretations to help her see a scenario from a different perspective? For example, if your teen complains about a classmate hating her, prompt her thinking. "What's going on in her life that would make her unhappy? Might that be contributing to her attitude toward you?" Instead of offering answers, pose questions without clear answers, giving your teen valuable practice in thinking through possible scenarios. That practice will improve her ability to make more accurate inferences about others.

Discuss what it means to be a good friend.

Because of your teen's new social sensitivity, she is likely to wrestle with some of the subtler dynamics of friendships ("Why is it we always have to go along with Gena's plan? Why can't I ever decide what we're going to do?"). Power dynamics in relationships can be confusing. Teens are unsure about the boundaries they need to set. Help your teen think through what healthy friendships do and do not look like. Talk in general terms or use your own friendship examples to avoid judging your teen's friends. Teens want to better understand when another person has crossed an inappropriate line—like talking about them behind their back—and then, what to do about it.

Model using "I" messages as a constructive way for your teen to respond ("I feel frustrated when you always decide our plans because there are other places I want to go with you, too."). This modeling will provide the language she needs to assert her needs while simultaneously growing the friendship.

Beginner Saxophone Rehearsals: Sexuality, Romance, and Relationships

Marry what you just learned about social awareness and anxiety with your teen's growing adult bodies, and you have a medley of sensitivity and awkwardness. Certainly, teens are becoming attracted to others. They are taking notice of others' bodies, personalities, and attributes in ways that size up whether they are a fit for them. This is also a part of identity formation. Teens not only have to figure out the answer to who they are but also who their friends are and what others they want to affiliate with in friendship or romantically.

To grow healthy romantic relationships, teens need to exercise a number of skills:

- Self-awareness (*What are my attractive qualities? What are my boundaries?*)
- Social awareness (*Am I accurately interpreting the subtle cues that she likes me or am I just making them up?*)
- Self-management (*How can I resist the urge to touch my crush in the hallway? or How can I deal with the embarrassment of all my friends knowing I like him?*)
- Relationship skills (*How can I truly get to know him and listen to what he cares about when I'm so distracted by my discomfort and his gleaming eyes? How can I tell him to stop advancing physically when I'm always uncomfortable and unsure?*)
- Responsible decision-making (*Though I have these strong impulses, which will I act on and which will get me into trouble?*)

Some teens explore by entering into romantic relationships in their teen years and others may not, deciding they want to wait. Either is perfectly normal for their development—and either can add social stress as they compare themselves to others.

Interestingly, teens want our guidance on what it takes to engage in and sustain healthy romantic relationships. Harvard's Making Caring Common Project surveyed a broad base of 18- to 25-year-olds in the United States about

Teen Relationship Questions

Though your teen may or may not pose these questions directly to you, it's likely she will be considering (even worrying herself about) the following.

- When and how do I start a relationship?
- Can friends become romantic partners?
- What if my crush rejects me when I try to initiate something?
- Will I always feel so awkward with my crush?
- How often do I communicate with my crush (text, Snapchat, in the hallway)?
- Do we hold hands in public, at school?
- How do I kiss a person for the first time? Where? When? How? Who will initiate? And what if they don't want to be kissed? How will I know?
- What if my friends tease me?
- What will my parents think?
- Will my body ever appeal to anyone? Why can't I have big muscles, a bigger chest, less/more…?

the conversations they had or didn't have with their parents and what they felt they needed in their teen years. Seventy percent said they wished they had received more guidance and support from their parents on what it means to be in a healthy, committed romantic relationship. When parents have "the (sex) talk," it tends to:

- Be a one-time conversation.
- Focus on the mechanics (the physical act of sex).
- Include cautionary tales or fears of pregnancy, sexually transmitted diseases, and drug and alcohol use and dangers.

But teen worries are not our worries. The adult fears we bring to them can shut the door on important conversations when we begin with our fears as opposed to understanding where their young minds are. Instead, our focus needs to be on how we can help teens create safe, healthy, and caring relationships.

Tips for Conductors on Teen Relationships

To figure out how we can best support our teens, let's get in their heads for a moment. Check out the teen's relationship questions (see sidebar on page 141) for an abbreviated version or cue up a John Hughes' movie from the 1980s, such as *Pretty In Pink* or *The Breakfast Club*. Here are some tips to help your teen with relationships.

Use self-management skills and empathy.

Use your own best self-management skills to enter into important conversations about your teen's questions. Share anecdotes of awkward first interactions. Over a family dinner, tell stories of first meetings, dates, and kisses. Laugh together. Who initiated what? What did the note in the locker say? Teens may not ask, but rest assured they're curious. Start the conversation in an it's-okay-to-feel-nervous-and-strange kind of way. This can open the door to supportive conversations with your teen.

Talk about the hallmarks of healthy relationships—first and often.

My Dad used to ask, "Have you seen him angry? Can he get mad without hurting anyone?" This became a litmus test for me in my romantic relationships. What is considered a healthy relationship to you? What boundaries do you set in your relationships that are not to be crossed? What if your crush makes bad decisions that get him in trouble, but you are deeply into him? These are complex social situations to navigate, and teens need to feel like they can trust talking with you about them. The more practice they have in discussing these complexities while thinking for themselves about potential answers, the more they will hone their responsible decision-making skills.

Preventing Our Teen's "Me Too"

Let's address some of our biggest fears. We know teens think they are ready for the thrills accessible to adults while we watch their impulsivity and incongruent judgments fail them. And, even if we trust our teens, there's the world to contend with. Our worries tend to revolve around date rape, harassment, casual sex, teen pregnancy, and peers who might introduce other risks (drugs, alcohol, or insert your worry of choice here). We fear online sexual predators. And what if our teens fall in love too fast, commit to, or even marry the "wrong" person?

The best way we can keep our teens safe in their risky new world is to ensure that they are in a trusting, caring home and school environment and have valued friendships and extracurricular activities (band, anyone?) that they love. Research supports that these are their best layers of protection. But there are also ways we can teach our teens to stay safe that directly relate to identifying and stopping harassment.

> "The best way we can keep our teens safe is to ensure that they are in a trusting, caring environment and have valued friendships and extracurricular activities."

Respect "Stop" and "No" as sacred.

Adults often keep tickling a child, or siblings might wrestle harder, even after an earnest "no" or "stop" has been uttered. It's a critical habit change we need to make if we are to model and reinforce that "No" should be respected. Voices need not get louder. Talk about this during a family dinner. Create a new policy. Help remind one another to keep "stop" and "no" sacred.

Do gut checks and trust feelings.

Teens continue to develop a language to express emotions. When faced with danger, they may more readily identify physical signs of discomfort first such as feeling nauseous. Practice doing gut checks. If you see an image in the media that is disturbing, ask how your teen's tummy feels. Make the connection between that icky feeling as a sign of danger signaling for them to get out of the situation. A teen needs to be able to have the courage to act on those safety threats while possibly disappointing or angering a peer or older person who attempts to exert power over him. If teens are taught to trust that feeling, they are more likely to leave a high-risk situation. Reprise.

Find the closest caring ally.

When your teen is in danger, she requires an ally. If fifteen-year-old Addison is cornered at a party by a boy who feels unsafe to her, she needs to know how to exit that situation safely while "saving face." In other words, how can you give her an easy way out that doesn't embarrass her in front of her friends?

In danger situations, teens need to learn to "look for the helpers," as Mr. Rogers advised. Abuse usually takes place when two are alone together. Though a perpetrator rationalizes his behavior, there is also a clear sense that it's not acceptable. You never want your teen to feel alone and helpless. Instead, work on identifying allies *before* your teen goes out. Make sure your teen has a pact with a buddy with a well-planned exit strategy to keep one another safe. They all have cell phones. How can they best use them?

Practice explaining truthful excuses why your teen would need to leave with a friend. "We need to go take care of her baby brother." Or, "We have another event to go to." In one Dad's exit strategy with his teenage kids, the kids were required to let him know where they were going to be. Then, all his daughter or son had to do was text him the letter "X," and he would come and pick them up. Anytime. No questions asked.

Promote assertive communication.

Mustering the courage and finding the words to assert your needs is indeed a learned skill. Doing it in a way that doesn't place blame or cause harm to yourself and others can take practice. Teens need to be able to express their hurt, anger, or fear and, most importantly, establish firm boundaries around what's acceptable and unacceptable. As your teen becomes more comfortable with saying what she's feeling, ask, "Okay, so you're feeling hurt. What do you need to tell others to protect yourself?"

Then, when our teens do assert themselves, we need to take them seriously. It can be tempting to dismiss a teen's upset because we think they are exaggerating. But rest assured, they are upset for a reason. Their trust in themselves has to first come from our trust in their feelings. If you are tempted to shut them down and move on, stop yourself and really listen.

Let your daughter practice speaking up for herself when you are out in public, even in such a small way as ordering her own meal. If there's a problem with her teacher, coach her on language so that she can approach her teacher herself. These small opportunities will offer her valuable practice in talking with adults and peers in a way in which she can assert her needs.

Keep an open dialogue about physical and sexual development and boundaries. Though we tend to shy away from the conversation, it's critical to keep an ongoing dialogue related to your teen's sexual development. It's as important as learning about proper hygiene. As they enter the teen years, boundaries seem to blur and their changing relationships become confusing. What's acceptable? What goes too far? Your teen needs to:

- Understand the facts about the changes—emotional and physical—in their bodies.
- Understand appropriate respected boundaries.
- Feel a trusting connection so that if there are questions or problems, they'll be much more likely to talk to you.

Question your family power dynamics.
How is power shared in your family? Are there times when one individual dominates over another? Is communication aggressive, passive-aggressive, or assertive? Your teen is learning about appropriate and inappropriate uses of power through your family dynamic. If you are not certain, ask yourself if there are times you feel powerless? How about your teen? How can you learn about new strategies to share power in your family by offering authentic choices and reflecting on the outcomes?

Be open to questioning authority and explain reasons behind rules.
Though you need to set clear boundaries for your teens, it's also important to recognize that they will question, test, and even break the rules. And as they do, they begin to better formulate their sense of what's right and what's wrong. You want them to be able to say no to an abusive adult. So when they say no to you, though it can be frustrating, it's important to listen and understand the reasoning behind their assertions. In addition, it's critical to explain the rationale for the boundaries you establish ("We set this rule because there is a major safety risk for

you. Here's why…"). There are always ways to learn more about a boundary. If your teen's curfew is set at 10 p.m., research together teen curfews, risks to staying out later, and related safety issues. Show your teen how adults make responsible decisions by becoming informed.

As we work on ways to prevent our teen's "Me Too," we need to remember that projecting our own fear on them to prepare them for unknown harms can work against our goals of prevention. Fear, after all, paralyzes. We want to build skills, empower our teen to speak up, and take action toward safety.

Become self-aware. Take some deep breaths and prepare yourself to start the conversation calmly. Use this as an opportunity to face your fears by giving your teen the skills you may not have had at your disposal. A young adult who is knowledgeable, who can assert herself and her needs, and who has open communication with her parents is far less likely to be taken advantage of.

Toe-Tapping: Impulsivity and Risk

Imagine Michael Jackson's "Don't Stop 'Til You Get Enough" filling the room with its energy and beat. Can you stop yourself from toe-tapping, swaying your hips, or bopping your head? The music sweeps us into a revelry of disco goodness. This is the kind of revelry our teens get pulled into as they impulsively follow their bestie to their next thrilling adventure. Impulsivity can be defined simply as acting without thinking.

The unique developmental attributes of the teen years creates the perfect blend of ingredients for risk-taking—the desire for new sensations, the need for independence and seeking out adult experiences, affiliation and comparison with peers who are seeking novelty, and an increase in dopamine (a happy hormone reward) when risks are taken. Whereas adults focus on risk, teens focus on rewards. Interestingly, impulsive decisions to take risks are directly associated with a teen's anticipated positive emotions—the reward. If the teen perceives drugs as a pleasurable experiment, she is more likely to try it. Similarly, if a teen is in a happy state, she is more likely to engage in risky choices, anticipating a greater happiness reward (and researchers have found that teens experience higher levels of reward sensations than adults do).

In addition, because of the teen's brain reconstruction, she has a tougher time learning from mistakes. Adults can make quick judgments about consequences, but teens have to spend more time considering the reasoning behind them to make *responsible decisions*. If teens do not experience negative consequences from poor choices (for example, if parents come to their "rescue"), they are not likely to learn that there are negative effects and will likely choose the same risky behavior again. These conditions make teens more susceptible than adults to addictions, including screen or video game addictions, which offer a regular dosage of happy hormone rewards.

Teens require risk. The good news is that plenty of healthy risk opportunities exist in the natural teenage environment without venturing into life-threatening territory. For example, our teens' first explorations into the romantic world—just saying hello to a crush—poses a high level of risk. Developing and managing friendships can offer numerous challenges. Teens are faced with academic risks, including exploring topics of interest and applying to chosen colleges. As teens glimpse their future adult life, they can face the healthy challenge of listening within to determine their sense of purpose if guided by a wise parent. Continue to prompt thinking by asking, "What do you deeply care about? How do you want to contribute to the world? And how can your decisions today move you toward how you want to contribute?"

Creative challenges can offer the highest forms of healthy risks, whether it's playing in a band, performing in a school drama, or writing short stories. Service can be an excellent outlet for discovering a passion, honing social skills, and taking risks. Traveling to new places and learning about other cultures can rapidly expand a teen's circle of concern and offer practice with social skills. Also, the risks of exploring the natural world can become a source of adventure and renewal.

Tips for Conductors on Managing Your Teen's Impulsivity and Risk

Teens who have friends (and do not feel socially isolated) and are engaged in extracurricular activities are far less likely to choose high-risk behaviors. Teens who tend to seek out and participate in unhealthy, high-risk behaviors were predisposed to do so through early experiences. In other words, young children who witnessed parents abusing alcohol or drugs, were physically or emotionally abused or neglected, or were exposed to ongoing toxic stress are more likely to experiment with aggressive, unhealthy behaviors in the teen years. In fact, only a small portion of teens engage in the largest share of dangerous risk-taking. These individuals have less resilience to stress and are more prone to impulsivity. For example, 18 percent of teens ages 12 to 20 accounted for two-thirds of the drunk driving reported. How can you support your teen in navigating risks and rewards? Try the following ideas.

Be aware of tempting with forbidden fruit.

Forbidden fruit syndrome is a human condition, not just one that afflicts teens. We all have a reflexive response to do what we are told not to do. My son will often say, "Don't look!" And what do I do, every time? I look. Cautionary tales may just elevate our curiosity. So how can we avoid it? Be particularly careful how you discuss rules and boundaries. Are you collaborative about setting them? Do you work together to learn facts to support your rules? Do you offer reasonable, authentic choices? If you become inflexible and unwilling to discuss a particular rule, be aware that you are positioning that subject as a forbidden fruit. It may just become the most tempting of all risks.

> "Since digital life can be a source of struggle, check the Appendix for more specifics about developing a family media agreement."

Practice delayed gratification in family life.

Self-control is learned. With instant messages, texts (no waiting at the mailbox), and digital entertainment at their fingertips, today's teens get less practice than previous generations with delaying gratification. Plan media breaks and offer wait times. Also, set family goals together and work toward achieving them. For example, will you work on eating healthier or getting into shape? Is there a place you want to travel to that requires saving money, researching, and planning? Work together on those goals. These will offer valuable practice in impulse control.

Talk about cause and effect.

The teen brain is ready to take exciting risks without linking to logic first. Teens have not had much experience with the skill of foresight, looking into the future to anticipate outcomes. But those brain connections can be enhanced with practice and repetition. So, whenever you get the opportunity, discuss cause and effect.

Tie it in to local news. For example, the neighbor's daughter wrecked the family car at the community park. Discuss how it happened and what other choices the girl could have made.

Open the door to healthy risks.

Teen brains require the practice of making choices large and small and experiencing the consequences. In her book *The Teenage Brain,* neuroscientist Frances Jensen recalls a story of her son wanting to dye his hair purple. Her question to herself when he brought up the issue was, *Will this have a long-term adverse effect? If not, then I'll support him.* And so she set up an appointment with a hairdresser she knew who would do a professional dye job. "Don't sweat the small stuff" might be an appropriate motto here. If your teen discovers a new passion, as long as it's safe and lawful, support it.

Create safe hangouts.

Yes, teens will gravitate to the house with no parent supervision if they don't have other places to go. Think through spots they could socialize instead—the ice cream shop, the mall, the climbing wall. Also, if you can, offer your home for friends to watch movies or play games, and then stick around. They can be themselves in your home with the security of your presence in the house to ensure that boundaries are respected.

Show your unconditional love.

Finally, make sure that your teen gets his daily dose of positivity, gratitude, and love. Consider that he'll likely get a daily dose of negativity through critics at school. He'll view the troubles of the world on social media. But how much love, connection, and appreciation does he feel daily from you? Even if he insists on his personal space, don't doubt that he still needs that sense of belonging and loving connection only family can provide. Parents play a critical role in making sure the connection teens crave is fulfilled at least in part through their family life.

Dissonance: Internal and External Conflict

Whether it's the paradox of seeking independence while still dependent, or the internal conflict of self-identity versus social-identity, or the pull between the risks necessary for learning, or the approval of adults, there are numerous contradictions in a teen's life. These conflicts can create stress and add strain to parent-teen relationships.

When your daughter faces an internal struggle, she may pick a fight with her dad to externalize her internal unrest. Or your son may scowl at you, trying to act tough and independent, attempting to reject the fact that you bring out the softer, more child-like side of him. These moments are the ones when we have to tell ourselves, *It's not personal; it's development.* It's reassuring to read about teen changes because the mood swings are put into perspective. *Ah, yes,* we are reminded. *This is normal.*

Tips for Conductors on Handling Conflict

Your teen will drum up conflict because he needs to push boundaries to further define his own limitations and figure out what he believes is right and wrong. His moral development will be shaped by how he can break rules, make mistakes, and exist in your family. How can you best deal with the paradoxes of teenage life?

Cover the basics—healthy sleeping and eating.

With all the growing that occurs, your teen needs healthy sleeping and eating routines, though these may become a source of struggle. Scientists have found that, on average, teens require ten hours of sleep per night. However, only about 15 percent of teenagers actually get that much sleep. The research is clear: Less sleep equals greater impulsivity. Sleep is responsible for consolidating learning, and organizing memories according to what was emotionally important during the day. The lack of sleep can create struggles with learning in school, as well as irritability and conflict at home. Learn together the conditions required for sleeping soundly (like turning off screens an hour before bedtime) and then come to collaborative decisions that are healthy for all.

Eating is another area where teens will want to exert control. Involve teens in food shopping, meal planning, and preparation, offering choices with favorites in mind. Learn together about guidelines for healthy choices so your teen learns about nutrition. Make healthy snacks accessible and easy so you don't have to face a "hangry" teen after school each day.

Prevent power struggles by offering authentic, limited choices.

Take inventory on the small choices you make every day. Are there choices your teen could make instead? Could you offer two options that would be acceptable, no matter what her decision? Delegating authentic choices gives your teen a sense of power and control with the added benefit of exercising decision-making competence.

Discuss and reframe self-talk.

We all have ongoing conversations inside our heads that only we can hear. Teens are typically unaware of the messages on which they are stewing. These internal conflicts can emerge as teens feel discomfort and decide they need to battle with you. So, talk about it. A client recently asked her fourteen-year-old son, who plays baseball, "When you're up at bat, what are you thinking?" Mom had witnessed his fearlessness at the beginning of the season, hitting every pitch. But recently, he was striking out, and his face sunk after the first pitch each time. His response was incredibly revealing. "On the first pitch, I think, 'I can do it!' On the second pitch, I think 'I'm going to fail.' And on the third pitch, I think 'Maybe I can wait for bad pitches so I can walk to first base." After that conversation, Mom encouraged him to repeat "I can do this" as he attempted to hit the ball. It made a significant difference in his performance. His face lit up, and he began to enjoy baseball again. And, instead of a fight emerging between mother and son after a game, they connected and, ultimately, he felt empowered.

Challenge thinking and then wait.

Because teens are just learning how to predict others' thoughts and feelings, they may falter. Challenge their thinking when you can clearly see it's gone astray, but don't force it either. For example, ask, "Are you sure Elliot is criticizing you, or do you think it could be more about him?" Let your question marinate. If you get no response, that's fine. You've provoked thinking and may find your teen raise the issue a week later. These kinds of revelations can become major shifts in thinking for a teen and play a key role in helping them through their social angst.

Plan for fights.

Every family fights. Families with teens may fight a bit more, considering all of the changes happening. Prepare for this. Talk about what it means to fight fairly and what is off limits in conflicts. Check out the Fighting Fair Family Pledge in the Appendix. The pledge lists five easy ways to argue respectfully and six types of fighting to avoid.

Guide to repair harm.

Perhaps the biggest contribution we can make in preparing our teenagers for navigating the world independently is with practice in responsible decision-making skills. Character is not defined by the mistakes a person makes but by how she responds to those mistakes. Teens require our guidance in helping them figure out how to repair emotional or physical harm when they've caused it. A teen's tendency will be to escape from the embarrassment of his poor choice, and our tendency as parents will be to yell or punish as we attempt to impress upon him the severity of his decision. But this will only deepen his shame and turn a teen to anger, self-harm, or rebellion—none of which teaches taking responsibility for his actions.

> "Character is not defined by the mistakes a person makes but by how she responds to those mistakes."

Instead of this traditional reaction, we can guide our teen to thoughtfully make up for what they have done. It's never too late to make a next decision that demonstrates care and compassion. Helping your daughter claim responsibility and take steps to make things better forms her identity as someone who figures out how to fix things when she breaks them. These are the roots of forgiveness and a foundation for healthy, sustainable relationships. To eventually commit to a life partner and someday act as a confident parent, your teen will need those experiences.

Singing the Blues: Anxiety and Depression

Anxiety and depression are concerns with teenagers. The simplest way to know whether your teen is experiencing either and requires support is to ask yourself, *Are my teen's feelings consistently getting in the way of having a regular life—meeting up with friends, going to school, participating in extracurriculars?* If the answer is yes, it's time to seek professional help. The consequences of not getting support can be fatal; it can be that important. And what if you're wrong and their feelings are just normal teenage adjustment issues? That extra support may bolster their feelings of care and offer resilience. No harm done. If you feel it's time to seek help, check out the mental health resources page in the Appendix.

Our Teen's Music

Through all of this, teens offer parents a unique gift. Because they are being born into adult life, we can glimpse the wonder, awe, and magic of being an adult for the first time through their eyes. If we feel a bit road-weary, we can enjoy our teens' fresh excitement and see the world of possibility through their eyes at the gateway to adulthood. The trumpets are sounding for your son or daughter and the chorus is asking, "How will you give your best to the world?" And we, as parents, have the honored front row seat.

PART THREE

UNDERSTANDING YOUR OWN INNER MUSICIAN

SELF-EXPRESSION

PATTERNS, FIRST AID, CARE AND MAINTENANCE, AND TONE TUNING

"Resonance energy increases in magnitude with increase in the overlapping of the two atomic orbitals [parent and child] involved in the formation of the bond, the word 'overlapping' signifying the extent to which regions in space in the two orbital wave functions have large values coincide…those will form a stronger bond."

—*Linus Pauling, American Nobel-Prize winning chemist and physicist*

"My mother!" I heard "Mema" Linda (my Mom) exclaim to herself while playing with my nine-year-old son Ethan. Some phrase welled up in her and before she could blurt it out, she caught herself. She heard the refrain in her mind before it was uttered. She was about to say something only her mother would have said to her. The content of the message, she recognized, was not in alignment with her own values. And, because she identified it as such—not her words—she stopped. It was a moment of clarity I wouldn't soon forget. She made a choice not to repeat the past but to become self-aware. In that self-awareness, she was free. Though my son was unaware, she set him free, too.

This is what it takes to become a jazz master, a confident parent. It takes recognizing that all of the interactions of our past are tightly interwoven with our emotions, language, and beliefs. Though we may be actively engaged in parenting differently than our parents did, the melodies from our past inevitably swell into our present. Some of those notes we are eager to repeat. But for those we wish to change, we only truly compose new music when we reflect on and examine the lessons of our past and how they fit with today's guiding principles for our parenting, and figure out how that translates into intentional interactions with our kids.

Children Raise Parents

In a practical way, children raise parents. All our social and emotional skills will be put to the test in differing ways through each age and stage of their development. During our toddler's tantrum, our self-management skills will surely be exercised as we feel anger or, if in public, embarrassment. When we witness our fourth-grader in pain over a friendship conflict, our self-awareness awakens as we recall a stinging argument with our own childhood friend and realize that we temporarily forgot but didn't forgive. And when our teen is arguing to attend an unsupervised party, our ability to project ahead, to weigh risks, and to understand what constitutes responsible decision-making will be put on trial.

Of course, we only advance our own development through our roles as parents if we remain open to learning from our children. This means we have to risk vulnerability—to not knowing it all or appearing perfect in their eyes. When challenges arise, if we point a finger and only wonder how we can change our children's behavior, we miss out on that learning opportunity. But with any and every misbehavior that angers, frustrates, or upsets us, if we look within and ask, "What do I need to model, to exemplify in my own behavior, that will show my child how to act with responsibility and emotional intelligence?" then we've opened ourselves to the schooling only our own children can offer.

Our greatest challenge is to deeply understand our own authentic melody—our temperaments, our emotions, and our core values—along with the new chord progressions that come with the blending and harmonizing we're attempting with our children and partner, too. As we become more reflective about our own beliefs and educated about development—our children's and our own—we gain enough mastery to resonant, to improvise, and to build up an increasingly complex, delicious sound that offers us deep joy, satisfaction, and meaning beyond our wildest imaginings.

Hearing Our Authentic Melody: Identifying Patterns

One of my clients, Amber, came to me because she noticed she was having intense anxiety for days over her eleven-year-old son Sam's social problems. "Why can't I let it go?" she asked. Sam was a terrific kid going through an awkward phase—making jokes, sometimes inappropriately in class, to get the attention of his peers. Amber worried when his friends didn't call or he didn't get invited to a birthday party. Sam seemed to not care for a while, but recently he had become more self-conscious. Had *she* caused that worry in him?

The moment Amber uttered the words, "I feel like my worry is irrational," I had my first clue. We began digging together into her family dynamic growing up, as I nudged: "Tell me about your parents and how they were involved with your social life?"

After a few comments, Amber hit on it. Her eyes grew wide, "My mom was super introverted, scared of social interactions, and sometimes wouldn't leave the house."

It's reasonable that Amber would have feelings of threat when her son faced social problems, since her training at a young age sent the message that relationships could be dangerous. Beating yourself up for an

> "Making the connection to the past is vital to deal with the present."

emotion that feels bigger than the situation merits is an essential clue that your feelings are unearthing personal history.

For Amber, simply making this connection was a leap forward; she began to build an understanding of her mother and her own feelings as a child, thus gaining empathy for her son. Added motivation to work on her reactions to Sam came from the fact that she did not want to pass along this family pattern of social anxiety.

Tips for Conductors on Self-Awareness

The key for Amber—and for any of us attempting to figure out how we live our own values rather than those of others—is self-awareness. We have to understand and admit that no one person has full self-knowledge. We make assumptions and have blind spots simply because we are human. Yet, uncovering those blind spots can point us to ways to more closely align our reactions to our hopes and dreams for our children. Let's examine practical ways to do that.

Look for clues.

If you find yourself wondering why you are feeling so intensely, that's your clue to search in your history for connections. Ask yourself when you have previously felt this mix and intensity of emotions. What was happening then, and how were others reacting? If your feelings seem bigger than the situation objectively merits, stop, reflect, and examine. Remember that emotions are created by each past experience—at any point in our past. They're not time bound. When you discover that moment when you felt that way before, get quiet. Take ten deep breaths. Have a pad and pencil at the ready. Then consider: *What is at the very heart of my upset and common to each instance I can recall?* Emotions seal in memories. Through your mindful reflections, you will likely be able to recall the story, even if from long ago, that connects to your present-day emotions.

Distinguish between "you" and "not you."

When you are clear about what childhood patterns—beliefs, attitudes, and actions—you want to change, consider the silver lining to those beliefs. Returning to your hopes and dreams for your child and how your parenting can promote them, you might ask: *Are there any aspects I want to keep? What do I clearly want to let go of?*

Seek understanding and appreciation.

When you begin to more clearly define you/not you, it's natural to become more critical of those individuals who contributed to the beliefs and actions you want to leave behind. Though we are focused on our parent-child relationship, we are embedded in a family system in which each person—roles large and small—influences our music. To support your continued learning, ask yourself: *Considering those family members who held beliefs I want to let go of, what conditions surrounded their life at the time when they were hurting me? How were they being hurt? How can I find empathy for their challenges by learning more (or, if they have passed on, can I fill in the details of their story on my own)? How can I generate appreciation for their difficult journey and perhaps lack of support or knowledge while undergoing pain?*

This reflective process can help set you free as you release long-harbored anger or hurt. Though your hurt may remain, this may help lessen the intensity of the pain by placing it into a larger perspective. Seek the support of a confidante or licensed therapist (who is trained to challenge your thinking and dig deeper than you might be able to on your own) to help you through as you try to make sense of your past to be present to your life. When ready, create a ritual to help you let go of any anger by writing your story or a message to your relative and throwing it into a fire. As you observe your story of hurt turning to ashes, imagine rising like a phoenix to a new opportunity to choose your reactions.

Manage the pattern.

Now that you understand why you feel so strongly and you have dug into the history of your emotions, consider your current life. What words or actions with your child trigger those big feelings? Write them down. When they happen, how exactly do you feel? Angry, shamed, or disgusted? Identify exactly when, where, with whom, and under what conditions these feelings occur. Understanding how these feelings are triggered is the first step to being able to take control of them in these moments. If we plan for them, these times in which we are challenged represent our greatest opportunities for growth.

If you have identified when these feelings occur and under what conditions, you will be quicker to recognize the pattern. As you begin to feel irrationally intense, utter aloud, "Stop." If you are in a public setting, head outside and then utter, "Stop." Repeat *stop* in your mind as your feelings and resulting reactions continue to repeat the pattern. Remove yourself from the trigger as soon as possible to shift your mindset. You might ask yourself: *How can I recognize the moment and stop the pattern from taking its typical course?* When your child is triggering your big feelings, you will need to follow these steps before responding to him.

Focus.

At the first chance, bring yourself back to calm. Go to a private space. Breathe deeply. Write down your thoughts. Return to a more focused version of you so that you are able to take the next step. You might ask yourself: *Can I feel my heart beating normally? Do I feel calm enough to think about my next steps?*

Tune your tone.

Now get out your blank page and write down a response to the following: *What do I truly believe and value? How can I show those beliefs and values through my actions?* For example, when my young child hit me, I felt hurt and punished. But my value and beliefs were that I didn't want punishment to exist in our relationship (either forced upon by me or him) and I could teach him to manage his anger in emotionally intelligent ways once I calmed down and refocused.

Ask "Who's the Boss?".

It can be challenging to define social and emotional boundary lines between you and your child. After all, you share a close relationship. Yet, his behavior must always be his own. Power must be shared. If our children are developmentally ready to try out an action, it's our obligation to let them, even if they do not complete a task in the same way we might. Parents must own their actions and offer their children the chance to be their own boss of their decisions—with the natural, real-world consequences that go along with that privilege. Also, if we have adult emotional needs, it's our responsibility to get them cared for and supported by other adults, and not ask our children to bear the burden of old wounds we are attempting to heal.

Composing New Music: Parenting to Our Unique, Carefully Selected Theme Song

Parenting can be our very own composition, despite other people's melodies repeating in our head. But, in order to do so, you must engage in creation. Consciously decide on a small act—new to you—that you are certain you can follow through on and realistically achieve. Ask yourself: *What positive goal can I set to react differently with my child when I am triggered by his behavior?*

Meanwhile, it's critical that you learn to manage your big feelings in the moment you have them so that you have the chance to turn patterns into teachable moments. Let's talk about how you can hone your own self-management skills.

Using Parents' Own Self-Management Skills

"I won't go!" my five-year-old shouted and began crying hysterically, running off to the basement to be alone with his anger. It was the second day of Safety Town camp, during which he was supposed to learn all about fires, transportation, and seat belts. The program recommended five as the right age, and my son, who frequently played with fire trucks, seemed like a good fit. But he didn't think so.

Because I have always planned my work around his schedule, I had a slew of meetings scheduled starting after camp drop-off time. After ascertaining that he wasn't scared of the instructors or the other children ("They were all kind," he told me), my temperature began rising as he continued to cry and refused to go. *What could be so bad that he's inconsolable about going to camp?* I wondered. I paced the kitchen, an earshot away from him, like a restless tiger. An inferno was raging inside me. It was a five-alarm fire—both mom and child flaming mad. He was clearly not stopping his angry cry. What could I do?

The rush of emotion we feel is only sent through our body for a remarkably quick six seconds. But, as we know, our heat lasts a lot longer. Why? Our internal story—the stewing and brewing we do—refuels our emotions. If you happen to react aggressively, either through raising your voice or lashing out physically (even if it's throwing a pillow), then there's an even greater surge of chemistry. Your reactions feed back to your body that you need more energy if you are to succeed in fighting the battle you have begun.

How could he possibly be crying for this long? I thought as I paced around the kitchen. My focus was on him, but some of it should have been on me, too. I was hopping mad, and my son could feel it. We were refueling one another. So often we view our child as wildly upset but don't consider that our internal flames add to our child's. Time for first aid!

Families actively prepare for the unlikely event of a physical fire in the home. We put up smoke alarms and practice exit strategies. But what about preparing for emotional fires? There's a certainty that every family member will be, at some point, taken over by anger, anxiety, or upset. Emotional fires happen in every household and can occur multiple times. Isn't it as important to have a plan for our biggest feelings to ensure the safety of our family members?

Unpacking the First Aid Kit

It helps to have a general sense of how your brain functions under great stress to know why you should have a plan. Anytime you are emotionally shaken from fear, anxiety, anger, or hurt, you are functioning from your primal brain, your amygdala. Chemicals wash over the rest of your brain, cutting off access so that your only functioning abilities are in your survival center.

Effective problem solving requires logic, language, and creativity, thinking which cannot be accessed when greatly upset. When your child makes a poor choice that angers you, if your plan is to come up with a logical consequence on the spot, you will not be capable of that kind of thinking. This "hijacking" of your brain, as Daniel Goleman, bestselling author of *Emotional Intelligence,* refers to it, serves a critical role. In true survival circumstances, you are able to focus on fighting, freezing in place, or fleeing from the danger source. But in family life, fighting, freezing, or fleeing are often not constructive, safe, or practical responses.

The brain requires practice and planning to be able to react in ways you want it to when it's taken over. If you surrender to its default (fight, flight, freeze), you may do or say something that you will later regret, hurting those you love. Why take that kind of risk? Creating and practicing a plan for what each member can do when he is in this state of mind can prepare all members to act with emotional intelligence during a crisis—large or small.

Preschool Pants on Fire

The description on page 163 of the brain under duress relates to adults and children alike. But consider this: The child's brain grows and develops from the back of the brain—the primal amygdala—forward, developing those essential connections over time through experiences that enhance language ability, creative problem-solving, and logical thinking (which we know doesn't solidly connect until emerging adulthood). Your child is more comfortable operating in the primal brain thinking space and may be able to hold out much longer than you with his intensity of feeling. A child's ability to sustain heightened emotion can challenge us as we deal with the rattling discomfort of lingering in that state of mind.

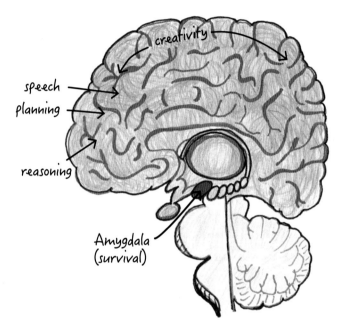

Establishing the Emotional Safety Plan

What does it mean to establish an emotional safety plan? Simply put, sit down as a family and talk about what happens when you get really upset. What physical symptoms do you experience? How do you know you've been taken over by a firestorm of feelings? What tends to trigger those big feelings? Is there a particular circumstance or time of day that is a more vulnerable time? Then, figure out exactly what each person will do to calm down.

Model this by creating your plan first. What will you say when you are overtaken that will cue your family that you are working your plan? Mine is, "Mommy needs five minutes." Short, to-the-point, and I use it every time. What will your body do? For example, I hold out my hand with five fingers splayed because I've got energy to burn. Then, where will you go? You may head to your favorite chair, or your bedroom, or—particularly for families with littles—staying in the room but going inside of yourself is key so your young ones don't get scared you're leaving them.

When you get to your spot, what will do? Mindful breathing should be step one. Take at least ten deep breaths when upset. If you need to, take more. Refer back to the "Stop, Drop, and Roll" plan in chapter 4 (see page 81). When you've returned to calm—enough that you have the mental capacity to form a considered reaction—you might ask yourself: *How will I reenter constructively?* Make a quick plan before you leave your calm down seat. Don't miss the template of a plan with these questions in the Appendix.

Simple Harmony Phrasing: Feelings First

When you've cooled your jets and need to return to the scene of the fire where your child may or may not have calmed down yet, how can you proceed confidently? First, remember the mantra "safety first." In this case, your mantra becomes "feelings first." Don't focus on the debated issue. Focus on helping your child calm down. "Would your teddy bear or your safe base help you feel better?" Offer a choice of soothing options. Then, when she has calmed down, continue with taking care of feelings. Acknowledge that she was upset and ask if she was angry or hurt. Discover her interpretation of what she felt and what triggered that feeling.

After you have listened and shown compassion for your child's pain, offer your own perspective in the form of an "I" message. In my example from above, I'd say, "I felt angry and frustrated when you refused to go to camp because I thought we had a good plan for your day." This is another buy one, get one. You'll model a way of articulating the problem while owning your feelings first. Then you might consider his trigger and how he might get his needs met, while also achieving your goals. In the case of camp, my son and I agreed that he would attend that day as a trial without assuming he would go the rest of next week. He'd give it his best shot and, if it didn't work out, we'd revisit the discussion. I made sure to introduce him to a few new friends and that second discussion never needed to take place. Ah, harmony.

A Return to Kindergarten: Our Daily Dose of Mindfulness

Recent research on what happens in our brains and bodies helps us understand why mindfulness can make such a significant difference in our lives as parents. To boil it down to essence, daily deep focused breathing or meditation lowers our emotional defenses (or returns us to our fresh "kindergarten state" in which we are open, receptive, and without ego ready to explore ideas). Because of this, we are able to better observe our own feelings and reactions to our children's behaviors, helping raise our self-awareness. We can better identify when our defenses go up to protect ourselves and recognize how those defenses can shut out chances to connect or learn from our children. In our mindful kindergarten state, we are able to become students of our children. We grow our self-knowledge, freeing ourselves of worn-out patterns and, in doing so, move closer toward the confident parent we want to become.

This commitment to self-care and maintenance is critical if we are to extend our patience to meet the parenting challenges posed at each stage of child development. If we are to notice, appreciate, learn from, and even gain joy from our children, our renewal is critical. Just as teens require enough sleep to be able to learn in school the next day, parents require mindfulness each day to truly receive the gifts our children offer us.

Tips for Conductors on Mindfulness

If you look forward to your morning cup of java, as I do, use that as your reminder to breathe. Create a ritual. Walk outside. Breathe in the fresh air. I read one page from an author who inspires me to think deeply. What wisdom nugget can you find? If you are a meditator, you have your practice in place. But if not, mindfulness doesn't require a vast amount of time and you will discover yourself gaining mental space and self-control. If done enough, the practice turns to habit. I find that, because I know the power of breathing to restore my calm, I will automatically begin deep breathing at a traffic light, or while waiting in line at the drug store. How will you renew yourself daily for the benefit of your entire family?

Actively managing your own stress.
Parents who work to manage their own stress in healthy and constructive ways are far more likely to be empathetic and patient with the social and emotional learning

of their children or teens and far less likely to get into the power struggles that can drive misbehaviors. Each age and stage comes with its share of stressors, making the full parenting lifespan a critical time to evaluate what you are doing to manage your stress. Create your own daily mindfulness habit. For example, maybe after school time is typically full of chaos as children return mentally tired, hungry,

> **"Parents who work to manage their own stress in healthy ways are far more likely to be empathetic with the social and emotional learning of their children."**

and in need of physical exertion. Before they arrive, can you take fifteen minutes to breathe deeply, stretch, and regain your calm center?

Modeling joy from creative outlets.

Have you wanted to take a cooking class but just couldn't find the time? Do you feel at peace when you put paint on canvas? Now is the time to pursue that creative urge. The benefits may be greater than you think.

- You are modeling a specific way you can feed your need for healthy risk-taking.
- You're managing your stress by engaging in a renewing activity of your choosing.
- You're discovering your own sense of independence as your toddler, tween, or teen simultaneously seeks out his own.

Learning about learning.

A frequent source of conflict between parent and child can come not only from the mistakes children make as they take developmental strides (as you learned about through the Ages and Stages chapters), but also our very own developmental needs that, if ignored, can well up in a pool of frustration. Just as our anxiety lessens when we learn more about what our children are tackling in their development, we can extend our own patience and self-understanding by learning about what we are undergoing. Whereas in our twenties, we were breaking away from our childhood home and forging our own adult identity with experimentation and adventure, in our thirties, we attempt to establish roots—in our careers and family lives. In our forties, we crave becoming the authors of our life and engage in deep reflection about how we can do that while facing mounting responsibilities and commitments. In our fifties, we begin to treasure quality over quantity, reaching out to others to collaborate, realizing we can't do it all on our own and that we will expand our impact if we become interdependent. Consider how this time in your life is challenging you to grow. As you learn about your child's development, what issues do you both face that could be challenging you? What issues are you uniquely facing that need acknowledgment and support?

Listening to the sound of silence

We all need to occasionally step out of the throes of current circumstances to reflect and gain a fresh perspective. In addition to a daily dose of mindfulness, how can you withdraw once a week? Take a walk in the park during an intense time? Or simply schedule a time to go out alone and engage in a renewing activity? Not only do you have permission to "leave the building," it's important that you do so. Make a regular plan with your partner to take turns withdrawing (since your partner will need it, too). Fuel your own sense of well-being, and treat your feelings and thoughts with the care they deserve. You'll return from your withdrawal with a sense of renewed purpose and clearer thinking to extend your patience and make sound decisions.

Call and Response: Gratitude and Grace

What is the feeling that you want to pervade in your household? For me, it's gratitude and grace. We all get our daily dose of fear, cynicism, and anger through the news, social media, and those "Negative Nancy" people around us. Some of this can spur us to care, or to fight for justice in the world. But we hear plenty of negativity. How can we serve as our family purveyors of positivity? Not only do we need to show and express that we appreciate the little things family members do but also that we believe in their ability to be the best of who they authentically want to be. How can we ensure that gratitude is expressed to one another daily? How can we give each other grace in our mistakes, mishaps, and misadventures releasing the small stuff and realizing we are all only human and loving our humanness? If we want to feel appreciated for the work we do in our family lives, this must be our call and response. How will you bring gratitude and grace into your family's daily experience?

Producing Family Resonance

In the hollow chamber of a guitar, resonance is created by the vibration of plucked strings sending sound waves through the inner space circulating within its clearly defined boundaries (the wood barrel). Several notes can sound at once at differing frequencies, yet, with intention and care focused on one another, produce harmony.

We have to open ourselves to our vulnerabilities to create that space, as our children do daily as they grow. If we commit to ongoing learning—about our children's development and our own—those vulnerabilities become a catalyst for our growth. We cultivate one another's power within and discover the feeling of resonance. We synchronize our words and actions more frequently because we are learning together. As we recognize that our children's feelings and our own feelings are manifestations of our minds, hearts, and spirits, we know that our intimate relationships depend on valuing and reflecting on them. We can find a fulfilling satisfaction in our parenting as we learn to share power with our children, allowing them a voice, choice, and ability to fine tune who they are and who they are becoming through our acts of unconditional love.

We sit at the front line of social change. With our understanding of how to cultivate the strongest and wisest in each other, we are poised to stand up and create a better world. Our opportunity awaits in the wide-eyed, ready faces of our children. We need not wander far from home to realize that we can be actively engaged in composing our legacy each day, fine-tuning the best of who we are in concert with raising the best of the next generation.

We—parents and the children who we love—are confident-ready. We only need to attune the love that we feel so deeply with our considered, mindful values, choices, and reactions to resonate and make harmonic music together. You've now heard the clarion call. What will be your response? There's no more critically important work in the world than cultivating our own confidence to raise confident kids.

"We need not wander far from home to realize that we can be actively engaged in composing our legacy each day."

APPENDIX

This section includes useful templates and forms you can use as you work towards building your confidence as a parent. Here's a quick guide to what's to come on the following pages:

- **My Emotional Safety Plan:** A simple template for parents to create a plan for what they will do and say when they are angry or upset.
- **Family Feelings Word List:** A list of feeling words that can be posted in a home and used as a way to encourage, expand, and practice the use of specific descriptors for emotions.
- **Family Media Agreement:** A simple template of a plan a family can co-create to place boundaries and guidelines around daily screen use.
- **Confident Parents, Confident Kids Fighting Fairly Family Pledge:** Five easy ways to argue respectfully and six types of fighting to avoid.
- **Book Club or Parent Partner Discussion Guide:** A series of conversation starters and questions to prompt dialogue around some of the book's hottest topics.
- **Mental Health Resources:** A list of organization names and websites with a general description for families who need to seek mental health support.
- **References:** A list of information sources used in researching this book and that may be used to follow your interests further.

My Emotional Safety Plan

I know that my children learn to manage emotions from my modeling. I recognize they learn from my reactions to anger or anxiety. Having a plan ready and rehearsed will help me model how I want to teach them to handle their emotions.

When I am angry or experiencing high anxiety, I will say...[keep it short!]

_____

I will use a physical signal to go along with what I say when I'm upset...
[i.e., hands out in "stop" position, or a time out sign]

_____

Then, I will go here [describe the specific place] to cool down.

_____

_____

When I get to my cool-down spot, I will... [take how many deep breathes? then, do what to further calm down?]

_____

_____

I will return to my family when [e.g., I feel calm and know what I will say]...

_____

_____

I will commit to sharing this plan with my family (as I would let them know about any new routine) so that they can support me... [When specifically will I do this?]

_____

_____

Feelings Word List

Post this list in a central location in your home, such as the refrigerator, so that you and your children can use and refer to it.

Pleasant
Happy
Generous
Pleased
Proud
Joyful
Understood
Empathetic
Brave
Excited
Cheerful
Loved
Capable
Confident
Safe

Body Sensations
Hungry
Thirsty
Aching
Energetic
Tired
Shaken
Calm
Hyperactive

Fear-Based
Scared
Fearful
Anxious
Nervous
Vulnerable
Lonely
Miserable
Depressed
Weary

Social
Shy
Outgoing
Embarrassed
Humiliated
Shamed
Unique
Weird
Uncomfortable
Clumsy
Pressured

Learning
Curious
Awestruck
Eager
Astonished
Surprised
Mystified
Passionate
Motivated

Attention
Focused
Mindful
Scattered
Bored
Distracted
Grounded
Unmotivated
Frustrated
Depleted
Renewed

Unjust
Angry
Jealous
Aggressive
Competitive
Vengeful
Disgusted
Irritable
Outraged
Neglected
Furious
Compassionate
Righteous
Reasonable

Unpleasant
Sad
Sympathetic
Disappointed
Dejected
Rejected
Hurt
Grief
Stuck
Heartbroken

Family Media Agreement

We will use media in a smart, safe way that contributes to our family's health, growth, and well-being.

Our media includes (list all cell phones, computers, gaming systems, and readers):

_____

They will be used in the following rooms:

_____

and not in:_____

Each day we will prioritize the following [note what activities like meals, play with friends, extracurriculars] will be more important than screen time:

Activity	Times	Places	Who Will Be Involved

We agree to _____ hours as the maximum amount of screen time per day.

We will use _____(a computer timer, a kitchen timer, phone alarm, etc.) to help us know when our screen time has ended.

We will NOT ever use media (e.g., during dinner): _____

Exceptions will be made when (e.g., someone is sick): _____

We agree that if we see something disturbing, we'll discuss it with a parent.

Check out: www.commonsensemedia.org for parent/kid media reviews.

Confident Parents, Confident Kids Fighting Fairly Family Pledge

Fighting is inevitable in families. It does not represent weakness but only reality. I know that the way we fight—what we say, how we say it, and what we do—can either deepen our intimacy or create divisions.

We, the _____ family, will...

1. **Plan ahead** for how we will handle heated emotions.
2. **Take time to calm down** before problem-solving.
3. **Take responsibility** for our own feelings and role in the problem.
4. **Move to empathy** and get curious about others' perspectives.
5. **Work together** to meet each other's needs and forge an agreement.
6. **End with love.**

We, the _____ family, will not...

1. **Use physical force.** We'll brainstorm alternatives so that children have other options at the ready.
2. **Triangulate.** We will not talk with one person about another when they are not present. We will go directly to the person with whom we have a problem.
3. **Criticize.** We will not judge or comment on the character of a person in the struggle but focus on solving the problem at hand.
4. **Show contempt.** We will not use hostile humor, sarcasm, name-calling, mockery, or baiting body language.
5. **Become defensive or blaming.** We will not point fingers and use "You..." language. Words like "always, never, or forever" will not enter into our arguments.
6. **Stonewall.** We will not refuse to listen, shut down the argument, or give the silent treatment.

We know that our family relationships will grow stronger through our commitment to this pledge.

_____

_____

_____

Family Member Signatures

Book Club or Parent Partner Discussion Guide

1. Why did you read this book? What were your hopes and expectations?

2. Were those hopes met? Did the book generate any new hopes for your parenting?

3. Were there any heart-warming confirmations of your parenting, where you felt great about what you are already doing?

4. Did you disagree or feel that any part was contrary to how you think or what you believe to be your role as a parent? Did the book reinforce that contrast or change your thinking?

5. Did the book address your greatest challenges as a parent? Are you viewing them differently or do you plan to approach them differently?

6. What inspired you? What challenged you? What surprised you? Which part did you enjoy the most?

7. What did you learn about yourself? What did you learn about your child? What was the biggest takeaway for you?

8. Did any of the information on your child's specific age range surprise you or change your thinking about his development or your reactions to his development?

9. After reading this book, what is one practice or small experiment you can plan to do in your own parenting? How can you set a specific positive goal? How long will you try it out? How can you plan to reflect on its success?

10. Were any of the suggested practices that you are interested in trying out in opposition to your partner's ways of parenting? How will you coordinate with your partner or discuss changes you hope to make?

Mental Health Resources

American Academy of Child & Adolescent Psychiatry (AACAP)

Definitions, answers to frequently asked questions, resources, expert videos, and an online search tool to find a local psychiatrist.

3615 Wisconsin Avenue, Washington, DC 20016

(202) 966-7300

www.aacap.org

American Academy of Pediatrics (AAP) Healthy Children

Provides information for parents about emotional wellness, including helping children handle stress, psychiatric medications, and grief.

141 Point Boulevard, Elk Grove Village, IL 60007

(847) 434-4000

www.healthychildren.org

American Psychological Association (APA)

Offers information on managing stress, communicating with kids, making step-families work, controlling anger, and finding a psychologist.

750 First Street, Washington, DC 20002

(800) 374-2721 or (202) 336-6123 TTY

www.apa.org

Association for Behavioral and Cognitive Therapies (ABCT)

Provides free online information so that children and adolescents benefit from the most up-to-date information about mental health treatment and can learn about important differences in mental health supports. Parents can search online for local psychologists and psychiatrists for free.

305 Seventh Avenue, New York, NY 10001

(212) 647-1890

www.abct.org

Bibliography

Introduction References

Albert Einstein. Retrieved on June 22, 2018 at www.einstein-website.de/z_biography/biography.html

Crane, E. (2015, March 13). Revived by the power of love: Incredible moment 'dead' premature baby came back to life after mother begged to cuddle him for a few last moments and ordered baby's dad to take off his shirt and help. *Daily Mail Australia.* Retrieved on June 22, 2018 at www.dailymail.co.uk/news/article-2992862/The-miracle-baby-born-three-months-early-written-doctors-brought-life-mother-s-touch-five-years-old-s-never-sick.html

Google Dictionary entry for "confidence." Retrieved on June 22, 2018.

Isaacson, W. (2007, April 5). 20 things you need to know about Einstein." *Time.* Retrieved on June 22, 2018 at http://content.time.com/time/specials/packages/article/0,28804,1936731_1936743_1936745,00.html.

Leclère, C., Viaux, S., Avril, M., Achard, C., Chetouani, M., and Missonnier, S., et al. (2014). Why synchrony matters during mother-child interactions: A systematic review." *PLoS ONE 9*(12): e113571.

Moore, E. R., Anderson, G. C., Bergman, N., & Dowswell, T. (2014, May 16). Early skin-to-skin contact for mothers and their healthy newborn infants. *Cochrane Database System Rev.* National Institutes of Health, (5): CD003519.

Chapter 1 References

Durlak, J. A., Weissberg, R. P., Dymnicki, A. B., Taylor, R. D., & Schellinger, K. B. (2001, January/February). The impact of enhancing students' social and emotional learning: A meta-analysis of school-based universal interventions. *Child Development, 82*(1) 405–432.

Feldman, Barrett, L. *How emotions are made: The secret life of the brain.* New York: Houghton-Mifflin Harcourt Publishing, 2017.

Iwaniec, D. *Children who fail to thrive: A practical guide.* New York: Wiley, 2004.

Pease, A., & Pease, B. (2004). *The definitive book of body language.* New York: Bantam Books.

Pert, C. B. (1997). *Molecules of emotion: The science behind mind-body medicine.* New York: Scribner.

Prochazkova, E., & Kret, M. E. (2017). "Connecting minds and sharing emotions through mimicry: A neurocognitive model of emotional contagion." *Neuroscience and Biobehavioral Reviews:* 99–114.

Chapter 2 References

Bates, J. E., Schermerhorn, A. C., & Petersen, I. T. (2012). Temperament and parenting in developmental perspective. In Zentner, M., & Shiner, R. L. (Eds.), *Handbook of Temperament* (pp. 425–441). New York: Guilford Press.

Bornstein, M. H. et al. (2015, May). Infant temperament: Stability by age, gender, birth order, term status, and SES. In *Child Development,* 86(3): 844–863.

Braungart-Rieker, J. M., Hill-Soderlund, A. L., & Karrass, J. (2010, July). Fear and anger reactivity trajectories from 4 to 16 months: The roles of temperament, regulation, and maternal sensitivity. *Developmental Psychology, 46*(4): 791–804.

Fox, N. A., Henderson, H. A., Rubin, K. H., Calkins, S. D., & Schmidt, L. A. (2001). Continuity and discontinuity of behavioural inhibition and exuberance: Psychophysiological and behavioural influences across the first four years of life. *Child Development,* 72(1):1–21.

Kagan, J. (1994). *Galen's prophecy: Temperament in human nature.* New York: Basic Books.

Seifer, R. A., Sameroff, A. J., Barrette, L. C., & Krafchuk, E. (1994). Infant temperament measured by multiple observations and mother report. *Child Development,* 65(5):1478–1490.

Zentner, M., & Bates, J. E. (2008). Child temperament: An integrative review of concepts, research programs, and measures. *European Journal of Developmental Science, 2*(1/2): 7–37.

Chapter 3 References

Durlak, J. A., Domitrovich, C. E., Weissberg, R. P., & Gullotta, T. P. (Eds.). (2015). *Handbook of social and emotional learning: Research and practice.* New York: Guilford Press.

Miller, J. S., Wanless, S. B., & Weissberg, R. P. (2018). Parenting for competence and parenting with competence: Essential connections between parenting and social and emotional learning. *The School Community Journal, 28*(2), 9–28.

Vygotsky, L. S. (1978). *Mind in society: The development of higher psychological processes.* Cambridge, MA: Harvard University Press.

Watson, M., & Ecken, L. (2003). *Learning to trust: Transforming difficult elementary classrooms through developmental discipline.* San Francisco: Jossey-Bass

Chapter 4 References

Beatles, vocal performance of "Cry Baby Cry" by John Lennon recorded in 1968, produced by George Martin at EMI Studios for the album "The Beatles."

Children's Chorus, vocal performance of "Accidents Will Happen" by Junior Campbell and Mike O'Donnell recorded in 2008 for "Thomas the Tank Engine" television series.

Choliz, M., Fernández-Abascal, E. G., & Martínez-Sánchez, F. (2012). Infant crying: Pattern of weeping, recognition of emotion and affective reactions in observers. *The Spanish Journal of Psychology, 15*(3).

Maitre, N. L., Key, A. P., Chorna, O. D., Matusz, P. J., Wallace, M. T., & Murray, M. M. (2017, March 16). The dual nature of early-life experience on somatosensory processing in the human infant brain. *Current Biology, 27*(7): 1048–1054.

Meltzoff, A. N. (1999). Born to learn: What infants learn from watching us. In N. Fox & J. G. Worhol, J. G. (Eds.), *The Role of Early Experience in Infant Development.* Skillman, NJ: Pediatric Institute Publications.

New Radicals, vocal performance of "You Only Get What You Give" by Gregg Alexander and Rick Nowels recorded in 1998, produced by Gregg Alexander on *Maybe You've Been Brainwashed Too.*

Parlakian, R., & Lerner, C. (2010, March). Beyond Twinkle, Twinkle: Using music with infants and toddlers. *Young Children.* National Association for the Education of Young Children, 14–19.

Plataforma SINC. (2013, February 19). Fear, anger or pain: Why do babies cry? *ScienceDaily.* www.sciencedaily.com/releases/2013/02/130219090649.htm.

Ramirez, N. F., Lytle, S. R., Fish, M., & Kuhl, P. K. (2018). Parent coaching at six and ten months improves language outcomes at fourteen months: A randomized controlled trial. *Developmental Science,* e12762.

Reschke, K. (2019, January). Who am I? Developing a sense of self and belonging. Excerpted from "Zero to Three's Critical Competencies for Infant-Toddler Educators Course Curriculum, Module SE-6: Promoting Children's Sense of Self and Belonging." *Zero to Three Journal.* Washington, DC.

Savino, F., Cordisco, L., Tarasco V, et al. (2010). Lactobacillus reuteri DSM 17938 in infantile colic: a randomized, double-blind, placebo-controlled trial. *Pediatrics, 126*: e526-e533.

Seidl, A., Tincoff, R., Baker, C., & Cristia, A. (2014, April 16). Why the body comes first: Effects of experimenter touch on infants' word finding. *Developmental Science, 18*(1): 155–164.

Shin, E. K., LeWinn, K., Bush, N., Tylavsky, F. A., Davis, R. L., & Shaban-Nejad, A. (2019, January 11). Association of maternal social relationships with cognitive development in early childhood. *Pediatrics, 2*(1): c186963.

Tarullo, A. R., Balsam, P. D., & Fifer, W. P. (2011, January 1). Sleep and infant learning. *Infant Child Development, 20*(1): 35–46.

von Hofsten, O., von Hofsten, C., Sulutvedt, U., Laeng, B., Brennen, T., & Magnussen, S. (2014, November). Stimulating newborn face perception. *Journal of Vision, 14*(16).

Winston, R., & Chicot, R. (2016, February 24). The importance of early bonding on the long-term mental health and resilience of children. *London Journal of Primary Care, 8*(1): 12–14

Chapter 5 References

American Academy of Pediatrics. (2016, November). Media and young minds. *Pediatrics, 138* (5). https://pediatrics.aappublications.org/content/138/5/e20162591

Daniel Tiger and Friends, vocal performance of "When I Get So Mad" song *Daniel Tiger's Neighborhood*, 2019, produced by Fred Rogers Productions.

Eldridge, L., & Hughes, G. (2018, December 19). What is a normal respiratory rate? *Pediatrics, 138*(5).

MacKinnon, M. (2016, February 7). The science of slow deep breathing. *Mindfulness MD*

Chapter 6 References

Baumrind, D. (1996). Effects of authoritative parental control on child behavior. *Child Development, 37*(4), 887–907.

Cole, M., & Cole, S. R. (2001). *The Development of Children*. New York: Worth Publishers.

Common Sense Media. (2016). *The Common Sense census: Plugged-in parents of tweens and teens 2016*. Common Sense Media.

Divecha, D. (2014, April 30). What happens to children when parents fight. *Developmental Science* blog. https://www.developmentalscience.com/blog/2014/04/30/what-happens-to-children-when-parents-fight

Duncan, R. D. (2009) *Family characteristics of children involved in bullying.* Retrieved from education.com on October 1, 2015.

Fisher, M., Knobe, J., Strickland, B., & Keil, F. C. (2018, July). The tribalism of truth. *Scientific American, 2,* 50–53.

Frankl, V. E. (1946). *Man's Search for Meaning.* Boston: Beacon Press.

Gardner, G. E., & Walters, K. L. (2015). Collaborative teams as a means of constructing knowledge in the life sciences: Theory and practice. *STEM Education: Concepts, Methodologies, Tools, and Applications, 16.*

Gershoff, E. T., & Grogan-Kaylor, A. (2016, June). Spanking and child outcomes: Old controversies and new meta-analyses. *Journal of Family Psychology.*

Good Therapy. "Famous Psychologists: Viktor Frankl, 1905–1997." https://www.goodtherapy.org/famous-psychologists/viktor-frankl.html

Gottman, J., & Silver, N. (1994, March). What makes marriage work? It's how you resolve conflict that matters most. *Psychology Today.*

Harter, S., & Leahy, R. L. (1999). The construction of the self: A developmental perspective. *Journal of Cognitive Psychotherapy, 15*(4) 0889–8391.

Kim, S., Park, Y., & Headrick, L. (2018, July). Daily micro-breaks and job performance: General work engagement as a cross-level moderator. *Journal of Applied Psychology, 103*(7) 772–786.

Presley, Elvis, vocal performance of "All Shook Up." By Otis Blackwell and Elvis Presley recorded in January 12, 1957, produced by Radio Recorders on *That's When Your Headaches Begin.*

StopBullying.gov. "Facts about Bullying." U.S. Government

Chapter 7 References

Beattie, L., Kyle, S. D., Espie, C. A., & Biello, S. M. (2015). Social interactions, emotion and sleep: A systemic review and research agenda. *Sleep Medicine Reviews, 12*(24): 83–100.

Biglan, A., & Cody, C. (2003). Preventing multiple problem behaviors in adolescence. In: Romer D, editor. *Reducing adolescent risk: Toward an integrated approach.* Thousand Oaks, CA: Sage Publications: 125–131.

Bridges, W. (2004). *Transitions: Making sense of life's changes.* (2nd ed.) Cambridge, MA: Da Capo Press.

Centers for Disease Control and Prevention. (2006). *1991–2015 high school youth risk behavior surveillance system data.* Retrieved July 22, 2016. http://nccd.cdc. gov/Youthonline/App/Default.aspx

U.S. Department of Health and Human Services. (2012). *Child maltreatment 2012.* Administration for Children and Families, Administration on Children, Youth and Families, Children's Bureau.

Child Trends Databank. (2015). *Dating.* Bethesda, MD: Child Trends. Retrieved April 16, 2018. https://www.childtrends.org/?indicators=dating.

Clinton, Larry and Orchestra with Bea Wain, vocal performance of "Heart and Soul," recorded in 1938 composed/written by Hoagy Carmichael and Frank Loesser.

Denizet-Lewis, B. (2017, October 11). Why are more American teenagers than ever suffering from severe anxiety? *The New York Times Magazine.*

Fulks, B. (2017, February 23). X-Plan: Giving your kids a way out. *Today Parenting Team* blog.

Galvan, A. et al. (2006, June 21). Earlier development of the accumbens relative to orbitofrontal cortex might underlie risk-taking behavior in adolescents. *Journal of Neuroscience, 26*(25): 6885–6892.

Jackson, Michael. "Don't Stop 'Til You Get Enough." Epic Records, July 28, 1979.

Jensen, F. E. (2015). *The teenage brain: A neuroscientist's survival guide to raising adolescents and young adults.* New York: HarperCollins.

Kilpatrick, D., Acierno, R., Saunders, B., Resnick, H., Best, C., & Schnurr, P. (1998). *National survey of adolescents.* Charleston, SC: Medical University of South Carolina, National Crime Victims Research and Treatment Center.

Martin, J. A., Hamilton, B. E., Osterman, M. J., Driscoll, A. K., & Drake, P. (2018). *Births: Final data for 2016.* Hyattsville, MD: National Center for Health Statistics.

Moffit, T. E. (1993). Adolescent-limited and life-course-persistent anti-social behavior: A developmental taxonomy. *Psychological Review, 100:* 674–701.

Pilyoung, K., Strathearn, L., & Swain, J. E. (2016, January). The maternal brain and its plasticity in humans. *Hormones and Behavior, 12*(4C):113–123.

Princeton Survey Research Associates International. *NBC News state of parenting survey.* Accessed February 2019: http://campaign.parenttoolkit.com/index.cfm?objectid=B32DD6D0-ACA3-11E4-B6B70050569A5318#Section_1.

Rosso, I. M., Young, A. D., Femia, L. A. & Yurgelun-Todd, D. A. (2004). Cognitive and emotional components of frontal lobe functioning in childhood and adolescence. *Annals of the New York Academy of Sciences, 1021,* 355–362.

U.S. Department of Justice. *Raising awareness about sexual abuse: Facts and statistics.* Accessed February 2019 on https://www.nsopw.gov/en-US/Education/FactsStatistics?AspxAutoDetectCookieSupport=1.

U.S. Department of Justice. (2000). *Sexual assault of young children as reported to law enforcement: Victim, incident, and offender characteristics.* Bureau of Justice Statistics.

Weissbourd, R., Anderson, T. R., Cashin, A., & McIntyre, J. (2016). *The talk: How adults can promote young people's healthy relationships and prevent misogyny and sexual harassment.* Cambridge, MA: Harvard Graduate School of Education.

Yurgelun-Todd, D. A., & Killgore, W. D. S. (2016). Fear-related activity in the prefrontal cortex increases with age during adolescence: A preliminary fMRI study. *Neuroscience Letters, 406,* 194–199

Chapter 8 References

Goleman, D. (1995). *Emotional intelligence: Why it can matter more than IQ.* New York: Bantam Books.

Acknowledgments

There are many who played a pivotal role in bringing this book to life. I am most grateful to my husband, Jason, who believed in me every step of the way and supported my choices, even when my dreams seemed far-fetched and required long-term investments from our family of money, time, and risk. He is my confident partner, bringing music (read: spirit) to my life daily. There is no doubt this would never have come to fruition without his loving support. I am also grateful to my son, Ethan, who is now eleven years old and has served as inspiration for this work since the day he was born. His very existence has pushed me to constantly learn to be better to deserve the role of being his Mom. I learn from his wisdom and kindness daily. My own parents, Linda and David Smith, also led me to this book. With unwavering love and support, they taught me to dream big and that writing could expand my world far beyond the ordinary, if I only focused on service to others. A big thank you also to my parents-in-law—Jan and Phil Miller—who have always supported our family with open arms and throughout this process.

My research partners, Shannon Wanless and Roger Weissberg, have served as both mentors and collaborators, pushing my rigor and excellence to align with a solid research base. Both did so with big hearts genuinely committed to making the lives of parents, educators, and kids better.

Tina Wainscott of The Seymour Agency believed in my ability to create this book before it was written. She offered a fast-paced, intensive, high-quality schooling in shaping a book that would connect with people. Our missions aligned from the start, offering transformational ideas that could make people's lives better. Thank you, Quarto Publishing Group and the Fair Winds Press team, including Amanda Waddell, David Martinell, Katie Benoit, and Todd Conly, for making this dream a reality and doing it collaboratively.

There were a number of individuals from whom I learned that influenced the content of the book: Liza Bloomfield, Annette Roberts-Dorman, Emily Smith, Megan Calhoun, Debbie Pearce, Lane Pierce, Rachel Kemper, moms from the Clintonville Moms Club, Tikeetha Thomas, Arina Bokas, Stephanie Beier Phillips, Kimberly and Mark Allison, and Sharon and Anthony Perez. Thank you dearly for your support! Also, thank you to the NBC Parent Toolkit Team—Jamie Farnsworth Finn, Esta Pratt-Kielley, and Gabriella Timmis—authentic collaborators who elevated my platform to reach a larger audience. Last but certainly not least, thank you to the *Confident Parents, Confident Kids* readers, contributors, and followers who continue to teach me what it means to be a confident parent.

About the Author

Jennifer S. Miller, M.Ed., is the founder of the site *Confident Parents, Confident Kids* (confidentparentsconfidentkids.org) and has twenty-five years of experience working with parents, educators, and other adults to help them become more effective with children through social and emotional learning. She is a

regular expert contributor to the NBC Education Nation's Parent Toolkit and has contributed articles or interviews to popular publications such as the *Washington Post, Parents Magazine,* and *Huffington Post.* Jennifer has a master's degree in education with a focus on social and emotional development from the University of Illinois at Chicago. She lives with her husband and son in Columbus, Ohio.

Index

A

Accidents, 75
Activity level, learning about your child's, 40–41
Affection, showing, 78, 137
Alone time
  for parent, 168
  for your teen, 136
American Academy of Child & Adolescent Psychiatry (AACAP), 176
American Academy of Pediatrics (AAP)
  Healthy Children, 176
  on screen time, 100
American Psychological Association (APA), 176
Anger, 27, 99–100, 162–163
Anxiety, 120, 138–140, 153
Appreciation for family members, 60, 83, 128, 168
Apps, calming, 74
Arguments, 127, 128, 152
Assertive communication, 144–145
Association for Behavioral and Cognitive Therapies (ABCT), 176
Attention span, 41
Authoritarian parenting style, 117
Authority, questioning, 145–156
Autonomy, 83, 92–93

B

Baby(ies)
  communication with, 87–88
  crying by, 65, 66, 67, 76
  cultivating social world of, 84–88
  emerging self-awareness of, 70–76
  experiences of a newborn, 68, 70
  love for, 66
  massage, 78
  rhythms of, 76–77
  sight of, 71
  sleep of, 70, 77–78
  soothing, 68
"Baby talk," 121
Belonging, 92, 93
Best self, imagining one's, 122–123
Biting, 74
Body language, 29
Body, symptoms of how we feel in, 28–29
Book club discussion guide, 175
Boomerang rule of reciprocity, 123
Boundaries, for teens, 139, 145–146

Brain/brain development
  Baby's, 66, 68, 88
  break for, in 8 to12 year olds, 125–126
  child's response to heightened emotions and, 164
  mimicking of feelings and, 34
  screen time and, 94
  under stress, 163–164
  of teenagers, 133, 137–138, 148, 149
  toddlers, 85
The Breakfast Club (movie), 142
Breathing. See Deep breathing
Bullying, 118, 119

C

Calming app, 74
Cause-and-effect thinking, 114
Child(ren). See also Middle childhood; Parenting; Young children (ages 4 to 7)
  acceptance of, 37–38
  expressing their emotions, 21–22
  inability to "shut down" feelings, 29–30
  learning about their emotions, 24–26
  parents' hopes and dreams for, 48–49, 50
  raising parents, 157–158
  social and emotional skills in. See Social and emotional skills
  teaching parents, 60
  temperaments of, 38–44
Child care, parental confidence in, 86
Childhood patterns, of parents, 158–161
Choices, 14. See also Responsible decision-making
  offering authentic, limited, 151
  responsible decision-making, 53–55, 124
  self-talk and, 93
  teen risk-taking and, 146–147
  toddler's independence and, 74
Clean-up songs, 75
Coaching, 58
Cognitive flexibility, 91, 93
Collaboration, 126–128
Collaborative for Academic, Social and Emotional Learning, 49
Common Sense Media, 115
Communication
  about romantic relationships and sex, 140–141
  direct language, 106–107
  of emotions through nonverbal, 28–29

"parent-ese," 88
promoting assertive, 144–145
with teens, 135–136, 142
through crying, 76
with your baby, 87–88
Competence, 92, 101, 106
Confidence
  definition, 9
  examples of, 10–11
  examples of what is *not*, 11
  as understanding and managing feel-
    ings, 12–14
Confidence in children, 9–10
Confidence in parents
  emotional competence and, 12–14
  helping a child(ren) survive, 15–17
Confidence of parents, 9
Confident parents, beliefs of, 12
Confident Parents, Confident Kids (blog), 13
Conflict(s), 52, 150–153, 167
Consequences from choices, 42, 53–54,
  114, 146–147, 163
Coping strategies
  for anxiety, 138
  during middle childhood, 121–126
  teaching to 4 to 7 year olds, 96–99
Creativity, baby's emerging, 73
Crying
  by baby, 65, 66, 67, 76
  as contagious, 34
  naming feelings and, 76

D

Daniel Tiger's Neighborhood (television
  show), 96
Decision-making, collaborative, 127,
  140. *See also* Responsible deci-
  sion-making
Deep breathing, 34, 97, 99, 138, 165,
  166
Delayed gratification, 148
Dependence on parents, 120–121, 131
Depression, 153
Direct language, 106–107
Disagreements, 53

E

Eating habits, teen, 150–151
Efforts, recognizing a child's, 106
Einstein, Albert, 17, 42–43
Emotion(s)
  articulating, 30, 49–50
  awareness of. *See* Self-awareness
children learning about their, 24–26
complexity of, 26–27
expressing, 21–22
history of, 31–33
identifying, 49–50
managing. *See* Self-management
meaning made from our, 23–24
myth of "negative," 35
naming, 76, 95
nonverbal communication of, 28–29
parents learning about their, 22–23
from past experiences, 31–33, 158–161
symptoms of, in the body, 28–29
understanding, 30
unlearning myths about, 24–35
Emotional competence, 12–14. *See also*
  Social and emotional skills
Emotional honesty, 124
Emotional intelligence, 22, 23, 51, 54,
  80, 163
Emotional reflexes, understanding your
  child's, 39–44
Emotional safety plan, 164–165, 171
Emotional skills. *See* Social and emotional
  skills
Emotional vocabulary, 21–22. *See also*
  Feelings vocabulary
Empathy
  encouraging in tweens, 123
  teaching, 58–59
  toward child's feelings, 27, 29 34
Ethical questions, guiding children
  through, 54
Executive function, 93
Exit strategies, 144
Experimentation
  by baby, 72
  by teens, 134
Eye contact, 33, 70, 71, 106

F

Facial expressions, mimicking another
  person's, 33
Families Fighting Fairly Pledge, 128, 174
Family Media Agreement, 173
Family power dynamics, 145
Family resonance, 169
"Feeling first" mantra, 165

Feelings. *See also* Emotion(s)
  awareness of. *See also* Self-awareness
  as contagious, 33–35
  mimicking of, 33–34
  naming and accepting, 76
  of new parent, 88–89
  from past experiences, 31–32
  "shutting down," 29–30, 102
  talking about, with your teen, 135–136
  taught in schools, 25
  teenagers handling intense, 138–139
  thought-infused, 93, 95
  as trustworthy, 30–32
  when playing with peers, 91–92
  Word List, 172
Feelings vocabulary, 79–80, 95, 172
Fighting Fairly Family Pledge, 128, 152, 174
Fights, family, 152
Fine motor skills, 96
First aid kit, 163–164
Forbidden fruit syndrome, 148
Fourth trimester, 70
Frankl, Viktor, 121–122
Friends and friendships, 138, 139–140.
    See also Peers
Frustration, 40

G
"Golden rule," 123
Goleman, Daniel, 163
Goodbye hearts, 109
Gottman, John, 128
Gottman Ratio, 128
Grace, 168
Gratitude, 102, 123, 149, 168
Gross motor skills, 96
"Grounding" children, 114
Gut checks, 143

H
Hand signs, 87–88
"Hangry," 27
Harvard's Making Caring Common Project,
  140–141
"Heart and Soul" (piano duet), 132
Heartbeats, connecting, 15–16
Heart rate, 33–34
Higher-order thinking skills, 57, 78–79,
  93, 94
Hitler, Adolph, 54
Hitting, 74
Home rules, 103–104
Hygiene, 145

I
Ideal self, imagining one's, 122–123
Identity. *See also* Self-awareness
  middle childhood, 113
  newborn's, 71
  of parents, 88
  of teenagers, 133, 134–137, 140
Imaginative play, 93, 94
"I" messages, 140, 165
Impulses, managing, 50–51
Impulsivity
  sleep and, 150
  during teen years, 142, 146–149
Inclusion, teaching, 107–108
Independence
  in middle school years, 120–121
  in toddlers, 73–74
Intensity level of reactions and emotions, 41
Intrinsic motivation, 83
Introversion, 11, 37
Irrationality of feelings, 32
Irritability, 40

K
Kicking, 74
Kindergarten(ers), 93, 95, 96, 103
Kindness, teaching, 107–108, 123
King, Martin Luther Jr., 54

L
Laughter, 125
Leadership, 54, 75, 137
Learning
  about emotions, 22–26
  creating positive environments for, 59
  from family members, 60–61
  from our children, 157–158
Limits, 53, 94, 114
Listening
  relationship skills and, 52
  to your child, 47, 102, 116, 135
Logical consequences, 163
Logical reasoning, 112, 133
Logical thinking, 114, 137–138
Love
  expressions of your, 34–35, 149
  interactions with baby, 78
  for newborn baby, 66

M
Making Caring Common Project, 140–141
Man's Search for Meaning (Frankl), 121
Massage, for baby, 78

Media Agreement, 173
Meditation, 69, 166
Mental health resources, 176
Messes, 75
Middle childhood, 111–129
  bullying in, 118, 119
  changing peer relationships during,
    119–120
  characteristics of children in, 111–112
  collaboration during, 126–128
  coping strategies during, 121–126
  social comparison in, 113
  teachable parenting during, 113–118
Milestone moments, 83–84
Mimicking
  others' feelings, 33–34
  relationship skills, 52
  womb conditions, for soothing, 68
Mindfulness, 97, 166–168. *See also*
  Deep breathing
Mistakes, learning from, 146
Modeling
  children learning about their emotions
    from, 24–25
  on coping with anxiety, 138
  discovering a sense of purpose,
    136–137
  emotional and social skills, 57
  emotional reactions, 23
  in everyday routines, 48
  with "I" messages, 140, 165
  responsible decision-making, 124, 146
  self-awareness about your feelings, 14
Mood(s)
  catching from another person, 34
  identifying your child's "go-to," 40
Moodiness/mood swings, 120, 132
Moral development, 54, 103, 112
Music, baby making, 73. *See also* Songs
  and singing
My Emotional Safety Plan, 171
Myths about emotions, 24–35

N
Naming emotions, 76, 95
"Negative" emotions, 31, 35
Neuroscience research, 26
Newborn baby. *See* Baby(ies)
New things, reactions to exploring, 40
"No," respecting, 143

O
Oh, the Places You'll Go! (Seuss), 73
O'Mara, Peggy, 93
Orphanages, study on children in, 25–26

P
Parent(s)
  acceptance of their child(ren), 37–38
  emotional safety plan for, 164–165
  emotions from past experiences of,
    31–33
  feelings of new, 88–89
  fighting among, 128
  hopes and dreams for their child(ren),
    47, 48–49
  identifying how child's temperament is
    different from, 39–44
  learning about their emotions, 22–23
  learning from their child(ren), 60,
    157–158
  managing their stress, 166–167
  mindfulness practiced by, 166–168
  modeling by. *See* Modeling
  overextending themselves for their
    children, 52–53
  patience and understanding during teen
    years, 131–132
  reflecting on lessons of the past, 157,
    158–161
  response to a child's temperaments, 38
  response to baby's crying, 67–68
  response to bullying, 119
  responsible decision-making by, 54–55
  self-awareness in, 50, 157–161
  self-management skills, 157, 162–163
  self-soothing practiced by, 80–81
  sleep deprivation in, 78
  soothing a baby, 68
  soothing a nerve-wracked, 69
  spent on screen time, 115
  understanding their child's emotional
    reflexes, 39–44
  understanding their child's emotions,
    26–28
  withdrawing once a week, 168
"Parent-ese," 88

Parenting
    adjusting to child's temperaments,
        43–45
    challenges during first year of, 65–66
    influence of emotions on, 35
    parents' hopes for, 48, 50
    past experiences influencing our,
        158–161
    teachable parenting, 113–118
Parenting styles, 113–114, 117–118
Parent Partner Discussion Guide, 176
Patterns, parents understanding their
    childhood, 158–161
Peers
    middle childhood relationships,
        119–120
    playing with, ages 4-7, 91–92
    social awareness of teens and,
        137–140
"People before screens" rule, 94
People, meeting new, 39–40
Perfectionism, 103
Permissive parenting style, 117–118
Pert, Candace, 28
Physical development, 145
Physical symptoms, connecting emotions
    to, 79–80
Play
    for 8 to 12 year olds, 111
    imaginative, 93
    during middle childhood, 111
    scheduling time for, 94
    as source of diversion, 34
Playdates, 85, 91–92
"Positive" emotions, 35
Potty training, 82–84
Practicing, teaching emotional skills
    through, 58–59
Pre-adolescence. See Middle childhood
Pretend play, 84–85, 93
Pretty in Pink (movie), 142
Pride, in a child, 60
Prison, study on children in, 25–26
Privacy, need for a teen's, 136
Problem-solving, collaborative, 127
Problem-solving skills, 53
Projection, 102
Puberty, 112
Punishment, 114

Q
Quiz, temperament profile, 39–44

R
Reading together, 95, 99
Reciprocity, 123
Relationships. See also Peers
    middle childhood, 119–120
    romantic, 140–141
    skills for romantic relationships, 140
    teen, 140–142
    of teenagers, 140–146
Relationship skills, 49, 52–53
Resilience, 28, 30, 85, 147
Resonance, family, 169
Responsible decision-making, 146–147
    building skills in, 53–55
    by middle school-aged children, 117
    by parents, 31, 53–55
    parents modeling, 124, 146
    romantic relationships and, 140
    by teens, 140, 142, 146–147,
        152–153
Risk-taking, 146–149
Role modeling. See Modeling
Romantic relationships, 140–142
Routines
    for babies, 76–78
    before going to daycare, 86
    for preschoolers, 104–106
Rules
    explaining rationales for, 145–146
    preschoolers learning, 103–104
    setting with teenagers, 148
    for tweens, 111, 112
Rumination, 101–102

S
Sacred objects, 75–76
Safe base, creating a, 98
Safe hangouts, 149
"Safety first" mantra, 163, 165
Safety issues, 114, 142–144
Safety plan, 86
School(s)
    dealing with children's worries about,
        101–102
    feelings taught in, 25
Schoolwork, taking a break from,
    125–126
Screens and screen time
    for children under two years of age, 79
    limiting time on, 94
    recommendations on time with, 100
    for tweens, 115

Self-awareness, 13–14
  Baby's/toddler's, 70–76
  building in children, 49–50
  definition, 49
  during middle childhood, 112
  in parents, 50, 157–161
  for romantic relationships, 140
  teen's emerging adult identity and,
    134–137
  in toddlers, 73–76
Self-control, 78, 94–95, 137, 148
Self-management, 49
  for babies and toddlers, 78–82
  building skills in, 50–51
  developed in children ages 4 to 7,
    96–100
  of parents, 157, 162–164
  potty training and, 82–83
  for romantic relationships, 140
  teen relationships and, 142
Self-soothing, 80
Self-talk, 93, 151
Sense of purpose, 136–137
Sensitive child(ren), 43–44
Sensitivities, in teens, 134–135, 139
Sensory sensitivity, 42
Separation anxiety, 85–87
Sexual development, 145
Sexual predators, 142–145
Sign language, 87–88
Singing. See Songs and singing
Skin-to-skin contact, 15–16, 33, 78
Sleep
  Baby's, 70, 77–78
  for teens, 150
Social and emotional skills, 47
  challenges that subvert development in,
    100–103
  decision-making skills, 53–55
  helping your child develop, 57–60
  learning with your child(ren), 60–61
  parent's hopes and dreams aligning
    with, 48–49, 50
  relationship skills, 52–53
  responsible decision-making skills. See
    Responsible decision-making
  self-awareness. See Self-awareness
  self-management. See Self-management
  social awareness. See Social awareness
Social anxiety, 120

Social awareness
  building skills in, 51–52
  cultivating in babies and toddlers,
    84–88
  during middle childhood, 112–113
  for romantic relationships, 140
  of teenagers, 137–140
  in tween years, 112, 119, 128
  during young childhood (ages 4 to 7),
    107–108
Social comparison, 113
Songs and singing
  to baby, 68, 73
  clean-up songs, 75
  during transitions, 105
Stoicism, 102–103
Stone, Elizabeth, 16
"Stop, drop, and roll" plan, 80–81, 98,
    165
Storytelling, 73
Stress
  the brain and, 128, 163–164
  parents managing their own, 166–167
  relieving in middle childhood, 124–125
Suicide, 121
Support network, parent, 85

T
Teachable parenting, 113–118
Teenagers (13- to 17-year-olds), 131–153
  conflict with, 150–153
  developmental needs of, 132–134
  discovering a unique sense of purpose,
    136–137
  emerging adult identity of, 134–137
  patience and understanding with,
    131–132
  preventing a "Me Too" situation with,
    142–146
  relationships of, 140–142
  risk-taking and impulsivity during,
    146–149
  social awareness and anxiety in,
    137–140
Temperaments, 38–45
Thinking skills, 57, 78–79, 93, 94
Three-year olds. See Toddlers
Toddlers
  cultivating self-management in, 79–82
  potty training, 82–84
  screen time for, 79
  self-awareness in, 73–76
  separation anxiety in, 85–87

Transitional objects, 76
Transitions
    for 4- to 7-year-olds, 91
    goodbyes, 109
    music used for, 105
    potty training and, 82–83
Trust
    building with teens, 135
    child care and, 86, 87
    interactions with baby and, 78, 84
    when learning a new skill, 56
    in your teen's feelings, 144
Trustworthy, feelings as, 30–32
Tween years. See Middle childhood
Two truths and a lie game, 24–35
Two-year olds. See Toddlers

U
Unconditional love, 149
"Use your words," alternatives to, 81–82

V
Vygotsky, Lev, 57

W
Wisdom, 23
Word List, Feelings, 172
Worrying/worries, 25, 47, 101–102, 158

Y
Yelling, 80, 114
Young children (ages 4 to 7), 90–109
    autonomy, belonging, and competency
        (ABCs) in, 92–93
    challenges that subvert social and emo-
        tional skills in, 100–103
    consistent routines for, 104–106
    coping skills taught to, 96–99
    developing self-control in, 94–95
    direct language used with, 106–107
    playing with peers, 91–92
    rules and, 103–104
    teaching kindness and inclusion to,
        107–108
    tips for dealing with angry, 99–100
    transitions for, 91